# MODERN HUMANISTIC
# PSYCHOTHERAPY

# Arthur Burton

# MODERN HUMANISTIC PSYCHOTHERAPY

Jossey-Bass Inc., Publishers

615 Montgomery Street · San Francisco · 1968

MODERN HUMANISTIC PSYCHOTHERAPY
*by Arthur Burton*

*Jossey-Bass, Inc., Publishers*
*615 Montgomery Street*
*San Francisco, California 94111*

Library of Congress Catalog Card Number 67–27947

Printed in the United States of America
by York Composition Company, Inc.,
York, Pennsylvania

FIRST EDITION

6797

FIRST PRINTING: *September 1967*

SECOND PRINTING: *September 1968*

# THE JOSSEY-BASS BEHAVIORAL SCIENCE SERIES

*General Editors*

WILLIAM E. HENRY, *The University of Chicago*

NEVITT SANFORD, *Stanford University and
Wright Institute, Berkeley*

*To*
*Edith Hamilton Burton and Vicki Ann*

# Introduction

Modern-day psychotherapies are becoming polarized along two broad axes: the behavioristic and the humanistic. Behind such polarization lie forces imposed by the patient himself, the conditions of healing, and the threatened integrity of culture. Scientific man, having produced the atomic bomb, is now under wide attack as blindly mechanistic and mensurational, as failing to pose the proper life-questions, as indifferent to man's inner being, and generally failing to provide a satisfying style of life. Humanistic man replies with ever increasing subjectivity, with the case for the uniqueness of all men, with the "meaning" of the individual life, and with the universal shadow that is despair and death. Western culture, in turn, defends itself and its prerogatives from revisionists while its children fall into the twentieth-century marasmus of nothingness; and the age of anxiety has now become the age of therapeutic man, in that overwhelming numbers of people seek relief on the analytic couch or its analogue.

The history of the humanistic movement in psychotherapy shows a progression from Freud to Sullivan to Rogers to Binswanger. Humanistic trends in thought, rather than technical advances, forced psychoanalysis to give more weight to the ego, which was done reluctantly. What this means is that the underlying currents produced by man's altered way of being-in-the-world became reflected in the deep relationship between patient and psychotherapist. But it was so subtle and involved in its growth that it went almost unnoticed by psychotherapists who took refuge in minor technical variations in their work and in cognitive evolvements of really small scope. The one exception was the psychotherapy of schizophrenia.

For Freud the narcissistic neuroses were not approachable by psychotherapeutic means. The data he cited in support of his contention included the patient's extreme narcissism, the depth of his regression, his flight from reality, and the lack of primary investment in anxiety defenses. Throughout his life, Freud implied—by letter if not by law—that an organic basis existed for the psychoses and that their substantive structure was on the point of discovery.

Those of us who suspended judgment concerning the ultimate causes of schizophrenia found enough in the actual psychotherapy of schizophrenic patients to formulate an interpersonal theory of the condition. One by one, the myths of Freud's narcissistic neuroses fell by the weight of the innovations of Sullivan, Fenichel, Fromm-Reichmann, Will, and others. The advent of published histories of treatment subsequently established that much could be done to change the patient's schizophrenic posture if two conditions could prevail during therapy. These were, first, the therapist's total absence of fear of the patient's primary process, and, second, a deep understanding of the "human condition" of which the patient was a part and product.

Since psychotherapy can in the long run only reflect the decadent social scene that the patient brings to the consulting room —and, so, too, the psychotherapist himself as a part of that same culture—it is understandable that libido-conflict as a wide explanatory principle for the neurosis, and the "couch" as the principal technique of encounter, began to fade in efficacy decades ago. Indeed, the patient no longer could or would stand for this form of lonely psychiatric encounter and insisted on more care, love, and intimacy than was given. In his indigenous perspicacity as a human being, the patient became less and less impressed with the intellectual juggling we called psychodynamics. He sought, instead, to become more responsible for his own decisions in treatment and for his life outside of it. Instead of insight he wanted freedom and release—the ontic step beyond the oedipal and castration complexes. And, interestingly enough, people of all kinds sought this not from the minister, the family physician, or the professor, but from the psychotherapist.

Humanism applied to psychotherapy may be a mixed blessing, as is true in every major philosophical reform. Some of the existential psychoanalysts, for example, believe that we can get along without an unconscious—Freud's great discovery. In still other instances, humanistic psychology comes uncomfortably close to religion in its exhortatory outlook, to philosophy in its preoccupation with ontology, and to drama in the clinical presentation of the individual life. To be a healer in the tradition of science, it is precisely necessary not to be a philosopher, nor a theologian, nor a dramatist. These disciplines may be humanistic in their own right, but humanistic psychotherapy is another matter.

*Modern Humanistic Psychotherapy* was in fact written to place the humanistic-existential conceptions of philosophy into a proper framework of psychotherapeutic science. It represents an extension of Sullivanian and Rogerian interpersonal conceptions to their widest and most modern manifestation in the cultural crisis that currently confronts man. Their work, and that of several others, anticipated, if not predated, Heidegger and Sartre, so that those who followed the former were not surprised by the latter. In this way, the evolvement of psychotherapeutic science follows a progressive and meaningful development rather than an extraordinary leap, as existentialism often seems to be.

Those interested in the cry of the "new patient" will want to read this book. Those interested in the "crisis of culture"—

as it influences psychotherapy today—will want to read this book. Those who want a new vantage point on the neurosis/psychosis will want to read this book. *Modern Humanistic Psychotherapy* does in fact:

1. Describe current humanistic/existential philosophical conceptions in an understandable way.

2. Systematically apply such humanistic/existential concepts to psychological, behavioral, and psychiatric problems.

3. Point to a new and more useful understanding of the neurosis/psychosis.

4. Offer certain technical innovations in psychotherapy with wide applicability to all theoretic orientations.

5. Offer treatment histories that illustrate the humanistic approaches discussed in the text.

I call the approach used in *Modern Humanistic Psychotherapy* "Being Therapy" because it interprets the neurotic/psychotic condition as a way of being-in-the-world, or, more correctly, as a way of non-being. All psychotherapy of this kind involves Being in the sense that the proper outcome of any psychotherapy is an enhanced or meaningful state of Being in which Eros once again assumes ascendance in the deeper psyche over Thanatos. The problem of mental illness I thus see as the iconographic one of "to be or not to be."

Those psychotherapists who have been somehow influenced by the humanistic developments in the field should be interested in my thesis. Even the convinced behaviorist will profit by the demonstrated understanding of the more than half of all patients who have no manifest libido conflict in the traditional sense. *Modern Humanistic Psychotherapy* admittedly "thinks ahead." Because it does, it becomes, in my opinion, a must for the psychotherapist and counselor who seriously reflect on their day-to-day work.

*Arthur Burton*

Sacramento, California
September 1967

# Contents

*Contents*

# MODERN HUMANISTIC PSYCHOTHERAPY

# CHAPTER 1

# Prolegomenon to a Humanistic Psychotherapy

Not too many years ago intellectuals considered a philosophy of life to be a necessary aspect of the good life. If, today, one probes for the essence of the neurotic's existence and asks for his philosophy of life, one must be prepared for a lengthy, laborious, and somewhat circumstantial disquisition that seldom constitutes a clear formulation of life goals. But if one asks the same question of a verbalizing schizophrenic patient, the answer is mute astonishment that the question should be asked at all. The reason for this basic difference between the neurotic and schizophrenic is an interesting and important one. The schizophrenic lives his philosophy of life; the neurotic merely discourses on his. The major distinction between these two kinds of persons is that one acts while the other merely thinks. In both instances, treatment involves compromising the philosophical

1

fixation to some intermediate point of functioning where life can become more meaningful and satisfying.

"Philosophy of life" as an exercise in rhetoric and debate is not new, but in modern-day psychotherapy it is coming back into focus, for this somewhat euphemistic phrase covers the meaning men give to their lives, or at least that meaning for which they search. The thesis of this book is that schizophrenia (and other psychic ills) represents an inadequate philosophy of life, one converted to symptoms and nothingness, so that schizophrenia becomes a way of existence—a way of being-in-the-world in response to the moral and valuative question: Why does one elect to continue living rather than to commit suicide? This is the fundamental question each man covertly puts to himself in one form or another. If he does not choose suicide, he must defend his psychological posture in life by any and all defensive means at his command. Psychosis is thus the last act of psychic desperation for one who cannot die.

The fundamental human equation for man becomes the transitive sequence—

Death $\xleftrightarrow{\hspace{1em}}$ Nothingness $\xleftrightarrow{\hspace{1em}}$ Non-Being $\xleftrightarrow{\hspace{1em}}$ Being

—in which the schizophrenic patient takes a psychological posture between the extremes of Being or Death. He has neither Being nor Death, and whether it is Nothingness or Non-Being which he elects depends on his special situation. If his self-organization is founded upon *affect*, he appears hebephrenic-catatonic; if it is *cognitive*, he becomes paranoid. Whether the manifestation is hebephrenia or paranoia, the categorical symptom represents only the external paraphernalia of a common philosophical problem of life.

It is more than ever mandatory in today's world for the human being to cope with the Nausea of Sartre and the Absurd of Camus. Modern life has become one giant trap of paradoxicalness. For a certain percentage of people the paradox can be neither accepted nor denied. It can only be dissociated, and dissociation is given a new and subconsciously more comfortable frame of reference. Schizophrenia, particularly in ambulatory and pseudo forms, is replacing hysteria as the "repression" of our times. In such a situ-

2

ation the therapeutic problem becomes not, "How do you make the self take up the social task?" but, rather, "How do you make the self *want to* take up the task?" Successful treatment involves helping the patient to want to become again a part of the human condition rather than accept a quasi-illness status, to want to accept fully Heidegger's "misbegotten and alienated world," and be willing to accept Nausea at least once a day. In language more descriptive than scientific, therapy amounts to tempting the patient back into Being; the true choice is between fully living or fully dying.

If the therapist is indifferent to matters of the logos, to human creativity, to ethical and humanistic questions—if he treats the schizophrenic at arm's length as a medical abstraction, and in terms of abstracted symptoms at that—he will find that schizophrenia is a mysterious and unclarified organic disease as well as an incurable one. And, indeed, this has been the history of the treatment of schizophrenia. It can be said that historically we have reacted to schizophrenia as to the plague. From the beginning of psychiatry, the founding fathers seemed covertly to consider schizophrenia infectious and communicable, and made protection from it mandatory. People who carry plague in one form or other are segregated by society and eventually end up in hospitals. A community of hospitalized schizophrenics is no community at all, but the infection is at least restricted. The state hospital can never be a community in a true sense but only a congregation of individually lost souls.

The magnetic quality of the schizophrenic's symptoms—autism, ambivalence, apathy, and associational dysfunction—were so fascinating to the founding fathers because they permitted themselves to be blinded to the more important questions introduced by these patients. The patient fully cooperated in the charade, in part because of the inherent tradition of European medicine, and in part because it validated the position to which he had been unconsciously forced by life. The Dialogue with the Self became socially more profitable than the Dialogue with Other. Thus a useful stalemate arose between the schizophrenic patient and the psychiatric physician which still persists today.

3

Sullivan sensed this, touched upon it, but did not live long enough to formulate his insights. Those he influenced carried the interpersonal point of view forward just short of what Binswanger, Minkowski, and others were beginning to perceive: that normality and pathology are of a piece; that life distinctions cannot always be made on a laboratory model; and that the mode one chooses as the vehicle for being-in-the-world basically determines how society casts one. Labeling, role-playing, and isolation function with great subtlety. Many inmates in the hospital cannot resist the label of sickness when $3,000,000 annually, a staff of one thousand, and a capital investment of $20,000,000 in the large mental hospital all stand ready to convince them of it. If the inmates are not convinced, the law can reinforce the diagnosis by its authority. The society that hospitalizes a bizarre, passive, nonconforming person who is hard to label proves nothing but that society is troubled by him and would rather not be. The proof of schizophrenic disease goes beyond "hearing voices." For more than ten decades, however, "hearing voices" was inevitable proof of schizophrenia. Rarely was time taken to establish the schizophrenic's life history in longitudinal aspect, and behind that failure, I believe, was the fear of infection of one's own reality.

This is not to say that there is no schizophrenia. It is, rather, that schizophrenia in all its forms has become so prevalent in our time as to make apathy, alienation, and ambivalence widespread. It is thus not so much a question of curing schizophrenia as of preventing those aspects of organized living which lead to autistic formations. Therapists have, I feel, sought the pathogen in the wrong place. It may be more profitable in coming decades to look for it in the organized social self, in the family, and in the unconscious protest mechanisms of social man which reflect the broader world in which the schizophrenic lives. Such elaborated points of view have permitted us to arrest the schizophrenic condition, if not to reverse it, as documented case histories reveal.

If schizophrenia can provisionally be seen as a condition of Nothingness or Non-Being, a total wasting away, so to speak, of

4

existence, then its treatment calls for a return to Being. Apathy and mania are both necessary responses to the natural laws of existence that demonstrate the pain of social nonparticipation. Delusions and hallucinations are simply phenomena of perceptual corruption fostered by the Non-Being state, and it can likewise be demonstrated in nonschizophrenics under conditions of extreme sensory deficit. For all men, the quality of existence is the same and only the quantity differs. The individual who has ingested LSD can be as schizophrenic as the most schizophrenic patient but he does not remain so because his sense of being-in-the-world is different. The reality testing process is generally in good repair in schizophrenia, and when the patient no longer needs his Nothingness or Non-Being the perceptual distortions vanish. I have seen such patients under therapeutic auspices return to reality in a very few minutes, although they cannot safely linger there.

In schizophrenia the self-core is damaged and there is a defect in the affirmation mechanism. Affirmation becomes curiously converted to its polar opposite of disaffirmation. Even in the patient's deepest disparagement of himself, however, his self-affirmation stands forth as, for example, in the grandiose quality of his delusion. People who in this way consistently fail to affirm themselves begin the everlasting search for perfection because its impossible attainment dramatizes their suffering and plight. The self then becomes weighted down with minuscules and its boundaries begin a variegated and ceaseless peregrination. As will be shown, this gives schizophrenic temporality and spatiality a porous and indifferent quality.

The self seeks meaning, value, and purpose. It needs to justify itself to its self. Its primary healthy manifestation is its presence: its stance and status at any single moment. The self is the active agent in the Dialogue either with it-self or with the Other. It manages the changes in the individual's history in relation to his present state of being and his future possibilities. The self is the moving force of the ontogenetic thrust; however, it also is reflective, and it reflects constantly on its own state. In Being, it is the successful

5

administrator integrating conation, affect, and cognition. In Non-Being, it is helpless to unify at all or to give purpose and tone to the personality since it cannot valuate itself as an agent of any kind. It is highly vulnerable to damage in that it seeks constant reinforcement for its own self-purposes, and this failing it falls readily into dis-ease. But it rarely gives up its potentiality for growth and function. It is capable of reversing apparently irreversible psychic states of decades' duration so that chronicity apparently is not always a function of self but of iatros as well.

Existence therapy is the attempt to turn those specific human aspects of treatment to the understanding of schizophrenia. It tries to put the biological in more proper perspective to the psychological. The treatment of schizophrenia has always been more humanistic than its theory, which is mechanistic, and those patients who have improved with treatment have done so on the basis of the practice and not the theory.

Existence therapy is now a technique, a very loose agglomeration of methods with a fundamental core.[1] It may, in a sense, be considered a technique of no technique. It can be thought of as a sensitive and intuitive accompaniment of the patient along a journey whose signposts are psychoanalytic in design. It is more direct, immediate, and participative than psychoanalysis, and its goal is not necessarily the resolution of conflict but the reinforcement of ontogenetic thrust. It offers to the participants not *freedom from* but *freedom to*. Its necessary treatment steps are: first, the acceptance of the burden of being man; second, the finding of value and meaning; third, the establishment of homeostasis through love and trust; and, finally, the creative discovery of Being.

When the patient has attained such a state of Being he is again free to choose and be responsible for his decisions. There can be no psychic illness when life decisions are made and responsibility is accepted for them. Confrontation with the self is the antidote to the denial which is withdrawal. Existence therapy, in my opinion,

[1] Burton, A. (Ed.). *Techniques of Existential Psychotherapy.* Palo Alto: Science and Behavior Books, 1967.

promotes that confrontation in the best way known to science. It is startling how quickly the conflict, and its somatic representation, loses the power to defeat the self, even when the symptom as such may still persist after a new mode of Being has been established. The feeling of release is equivalent to denying the conflict its instrumental value to demean and delimit.

Being is involved in laughter and play. Schizophrenics do not laugh, and they do not play until they recover their Being; their first sign of well-being is often a deep laugh. The play of schizophrenics is grotesque, rigid, and unlawful. They cannot seem to abide by the rules of play, or to understand the spontaneity required. More precisely, they cannot accept the metamessage that the game is not real. When murder or "leaving-the-field" becomes possible in play, it ceases by definition to be play. Psychotherapy with schizophrenics often is like learning to play again, although it has a "Russian roulette" quality in that any single move has the potentiality of canceling the total event. Families with schizophrenic members similarly have critical trigger mechanisms, so that the therapist very often feels he is walking on eggshells. Laughter, that is self-laughter, breaks the vicious existential circle because by laughing one steps momentarily aside, observes the self, and finds humor in what was previously grim. The paradox which trapped the self becomes open and no longer paradoxical by virtue of the humor of its incompatibility. The psyche thus siphons off the defeat of the self by this useful mechanism. Not many of the therapists I know tell jokes to their schizophrenic patients, but should a patient laugh at jokes one knows that it is time to consider the termination of treatment.

The chapters that follow are designed to look at schizophrenia from a more humanistic point of view than is currently the rule, and to stress the inner, subjective, and unconscious valuative process of the self. This vantage point has made possible a new approach to schizophrenia, as well as more successful treatment efforts than have heretofore been known.

PART I

---

PHENOMENOLOGICAL ASPECTS

# CHAPTER 2

# Schizophrenia and Existence

Recent developments in the psychotherapy of schizophrenia have led to a direct confrontation of the schizophrenic's mode of existence. It is becoming apparent that schizophrenia is a total reaction to a life situation which encompasses inner and outer worlds. The treatment of such a condition requires a deep insight into this unique way of being-in-the-world, and a commitment by the therapist to participate in the schizophrenic's "field." I will attempt to show that the problem of schizophrenic existence is related to the problem of existence of all mankind; that its treatment, and prevention, is theoretically organized according to certain philosophical constructs; and that the many psychotherapies of schizophrenia can be integrated within an inclusive theoretical formulation.

The problem of schizophrenia is the problem of reality, of the progression and regression that are dynamic stages in the flow of life toward some end. Reality must be dealt with in some way by each person, and the characteristic way in which one does this when direct confrontation is impossible represents substitutes or compromises that one finds more promising. The schizophrenic, however, presents such an extreme withdrawal from the world, and consequent distortion of reality, as to require a more fundamental understanding of the protection the defense affords. I have conceptualized the defensive aspects of the schizophrenic situation in terms of five vectors. These are probably not causal, but rather represent the character of the schizophrenic's being-in-the-world.

(1) The schizophrenic is at once the most omnipotent and the most helpless of persons. His every act carries the implication of godlike beneficence or wanton destruction, and he is both the donor and recipient of good and evil. He is never certain whether he will create or destroy, or whether he will be created or destroyed. Thus every gesture of love carries a metamessage that is unbearably threatening. The therapist who offers genuine love to him is puzzled by such an attitude. The schizophrenic acts as though his existence can be justified to humanity only if someone else were to give up his own place in the world. He literally fears not only his own destruction but the destruction of those who love him, and this is why he is so difficult to get into therapy.

The schizophrenic's feeling of omnipotence is comforting. No harm can come to one who is omnipotent, for all answers are lodged within oneself. Conversely, one who is completely helpless is also safe. The need for power or submission is deeply rooted and everyone unconsciously strives to orient himself toward one pole; it is only the person who is neither omnipotent nor completely helpless who is unable to retire from life. The schizophrenic's omnipotence and helplessness are not a chance answer to a need; Jung has convincingly demonstrated how the attempt to gain omnipotence operates throughout human history in myth and symbol. The schizophrenic draws upon the available archetypal remnants of both individual and racial attempts to survive. His omnipotent and denigrating feelings critically involve the therapist, and the therapist's own feelings of omnipotence and helplessness engage those of the patient. It is the therapist's demonstration of his own suffering and his resolution of reality between the two polarities that is convincing to the schizophrenic.

(2) At the personality root of the schizophrenic is a psychosexual disturbance: a lack of sexual identity. The neurotic has a sexuality, but it is repressed. The schizophrenic, on the other hand, has no clear sexuality: In the psychic representation of self, he is neither male nor female, but androgynous. Society expects sexual definition, and seeks it in cosmetics, fashion, and other props. If the average American woman were suddenly stripped of her cosmetics, perfumes, figure supports, and other sexual aids, she would no longer feel like a woman, but neither would she admit to feeling like a male. She would have no sexual posture in society. It is not difficult to understand why female schizophrenics have such a desperate need to give birth and thus create something, since giving birth is not only the hallmark of the feminine principle, but of individual worth.

Because the schizophrenic lacks sexual definition, he will distort his sexual reality. He will heighten and diminish it in all sorts of fantastic ways, as well as change its object. He will test the repertory which his body and his fantasy permit, but in the end he will find his solutions wanting. He will look to the therapist as the medium for his sexual growth and resent the therapist's security in his own sexuality. He will want to borrow it, to make use of it, but always with a sense of being judged for it.

(3) The impairment of the formal language and imaginal structure of the schizophrenic is well documented, and it is often employed diagnostically as the hallmark of the condition. An economic principle that seems to have some implications for the schizophrenic is that the organization of communication never exceeds what it is designed to serve. There is no communication where there is nothing to communicate; what finally emerges meets biological and social needs. The schizophrenic needs only paleological communication, for it serves his purpose well and anything more is threatening. Only when he encounters people unlike himself, the therapist for example, is it implied that his conceptualizations are

13

inadequate, as indeed they are. A chronically regressed schizophrenic may suddenly begin to communicate in a socially normative way, only to relapse again in the next moment. The experience of every psychotherapist seems to confirm that when higher levels of communication have existential meaning for the schizophrenic he will adopt them.

Probably more investigation has gone into the thinking structure of the schizophrenic than into the remainder of him. This, I believe, is more a function of the investigator's needs than of the patient's. The therapist holds secure to intellectual things and insists that the patient communicate with him in intellectual terms. But the schizophrenic seeks a meaning in his existence in relationship to a world of people and is not in quest of precise or logical thinking as such.

(4) The vector of "ethical sense" encompasses a variety of interpersonal phenomena. This sense draws together the various bases for the individual's response to culture, that is, to other people in his life space. All men experience loneliness and feel a need for love, which assumes the need to offer love in return. For the schizophrenic the loving situation is compounded and almost all psychotherapists regard it as critical. Frieda Fromm-Reichmann, for example, recognizes this when she says[1]:

> Psychoanalysis discovered that the schizophrenic could easily be encouraged partly to abandon his state of only seemingly self-sufficient withdrawal. This could be accomplished if he was approached by a psychiatrist who knew that the patient's longing for interpersonal contact was just as intense as his fear of it, which had originally driven him into a state of regression and withdrawal. That is, an intensely charged relationship could be established between the schizophrenic patient and the psychiatrist.

[1] Fromm-Reichmann, Frieda. "Some Aspects of Psychoanalytic Psychotherapy with Schizophrenics." In *Psychotherapy with Schizophrenics,* Brody, E. B. and Redlich, F. C. (Eds.). New York: International Universities Press, 1952.

Sechehaye, similarly, sees schizophrenia as a predominantly oral, that is, nurturant, problem, and proceeds to supply a more loving mother replica.

Culture embodies a system of ethics which defines interactional relationships in terms of their humanitarian, hedonistic, and aesthetic qualities. For example, culture promotes and proscribes the conditions of love and is constantly preoccupied with it. It provides both subtle and overt rewards for those who can love, and punishment for those who cannot. Punishment, in this sense, is a poor word, for culture is often benevolent in a punishing way, and its sanctions are extremely complex. The schizophrenic cannot love conventionally, or needs more sustained love than others, and so becomes a marginal person. His segregation for treatment makes society more comfortable, for few people can stand the constant drain of demanded love.

*Love* is an unsatisfactory word, analogous to the word *sex* which as Freud discovered went through elaborate vicissitudes in usage. But there is a long history of the concept of love in religion, the arts, philosophy, and human relations generally. No other word can describe that special transcending quality in human relationships which clothes existence in a framework of purpose. Schizophrenics lack an ethical sense, a continuity and identity with their culture, because the loving quality is absent, or blocked, in them. I hope to show this more clearly in its etiological sense when I discuss Camus' ideas. The lack of an ethical sense makes for the estrangement and loneliness so characteristic of the schizophrenic. Any psychotherapeutic attempt to alter this state must cope with it in a significant way. Offering a form of communion to a person who has no available loving basis for relatedness gives rise to special technical problems in treatment.

(5) Finally, the fifth vector posits a psychical and physical integration which is the bedrock of unity and organization in behavior. Little has been written about the schizophrenic's conception of his body. It is known that the body image of the schizophrenic

15

differs from that of the nonschizophrenic,[2] and that as he improves his body image changes and becomes organized.[3] The somatic delusions and the oral and anal displacements are meaningful for the schizophrenic. Freud has demonstrated the development of the erogenous zones and their import for character. It is clear that the higher levels of psychic integration are dependent on the lower or somatic levels, and that confusion in one is mirrored in the other. The schizophrenic presents an extension as it were of normal failures of body integration. Rejection by a schizophrenogenic mother results in the child's lack of her introjection, including the introjection of the body image. The child cannot come to distinguish the "love-giving" and "love-receiving" areas of his body from his mother. The sensory response to oral, anal, and phallic stimulation is not equated with love; there must be an intent to love, together with the proper sensation. The largest and most generous breast is as nothing if it is not offered in a sense of communion. The schizophrenic cannot in adulthood, then, nourish and be nourished without a bodily imagined counterpart.

Very little is known about this area of schizophrenia, but even in the present state of knowledge, apparently successful attempts to deal directly with the body image have been made in a few instances with children.[4] The alteration of the body image of the schizophrenic is an accompaniment of the psychotherapy that is mediated by the intactness of the psychotherapist's own body image and his body language. The patient reexperiences the nurturing resources of his own body when he can reencounter, within a loving framework, those who have such bodily resources. The desperate need of schizophrenic women to give birth is one body

[2] Schilder, P. *The Image and Appearance of the Human Body*. London: Kegan Paul, 1935.

[3] Häfner, H. "A Case of Pseudo-Neurotic Schizophrenia." In *Case Studies in Counseling and Psychotherapy*. Englewood Cliffs: Prentice-Hall, 1959, pp. 282–308.

[4] Des Lauriers, A. M. "Structural Approach in the Therapy of Childhood Schizophrenia." Paper presented to the 1957 meeting of the American Orthopsychiatric Association.

image need among others. It is the basic image of one intact self producing another, at once the most symbolic and the most universal need of mankind.

The nature of the schizophrenic's existence as I have described it has been suggested in the novels of Albert Camus. In such works as *The Outsider*[5] and *The Fall*[6] the protagonists seem to be caught up in the toils of an existence not unlike that found in patients called schizophrenic. In order to verify my own impression, I asked several psychiatrists to diagnose the heroes in these books independently. Invariably, they were called schizophrenic or schizophrenic-like.

Meursault in *The Outsider* receives a telegram informing him that his mother has died in a home for the aged. While he has provided her with the physical necessities of life, such as placing her in the home where "she can be with her kind," she has not often been in his thoughts, and he does not feel the "normal" sense of reverence for her. Although he wonders whether he should leave his employment to go to her funeral, he does go but he impresses the management at the home as showing a certain aloofness toward his mother's death and he does not weep.

After the funeral, he meets a girl and starts a love affair with her. Although she comes to love him and wants to marry him, he is indifferent, feeling simply that marriage doesn't matter one way or another and is hardly worth the energy of a decision. Later in the book, he kills an Arab in a quarrel not his own; his first shot kills the man, but he fires four more shots into him. Placed on trial, he reacts with a strange equanimity to his plight. He is without regret, and refuses to justify himself or to accept absolution through God, even when he is condemned to death. He accepts the reality of the world as he finds it and refuses to blind himself with subterfuges as other men do. Meursault describes the prosecutor, who, in

[5] Camus, A. *The Outsider*. London: Hamish Hamilton, 1946. This work is also known in English as *The Stranger*, from the original French, *L'Etranger*.

[6] Camus, A. *The Fall*. New York: Knopf, 1957.

17

summing up his case, said that he had studied Meursault's soul closely and had found a blank, " 'literally nothing, gentlemen of the jury.' Really, he said, I [Meursault] had no soul, there was nothing human about me, not one of those moral qualities which normal men possess had any place in my mentality. 'No doubt,' he added, 'we should not reproach him with this. We cannot blame a man for lacking what it was never in his power to acquire.' " Prior to this Meursault had listened and thought, ". . . I'd have liked to have a chance of explaining to him, in a quite friendly, almost affectionate way, that I have never been able to regret anything in all my life. I've always been far too much absorbed in the present moment, or the immediate future, to think back."

Another protagonist of Camus', Clamence, sits in the bar called Mexico City, in Amsterdam, and tells the stranger drinking beside him the story of his life—of his Fall. Once he was the foremost criminal lawyer of Paris. He was successful in all his cases; women were powerless to refuse him; he made friends instantly; and money was absolutely of no problem to him. He had attained what modern man views as the pinnacle of success. Then one day doubts began to creep into his closed system. He began to feel guilty about ignoring the call of a woman who had jumped into the Seine and drowned when he might have rescued her. His efficiency as a lawyer deteriorated so that he had to give up his practice. He lost his friends, his women, and his money. He heard a voice constantly laughing at him but he could never locate it. He went to desperate ends to avoid the laughter and finally could do so only by becoming what he called a judge-penitent. He says:

I am for any theory that refuses to grant man innocence and for any practice that treats him as guilty. . . . freedom is . . . a chore, . . . and a long distance race, quite solitary and very exhausting. No champagne, no friends raising their glasses as they look at you affectionately. Alone in a forbidding room, alone in the prisoner's box before the judges, and alone to decide in the face of oneself or in the face of others' judgment. At the end of all freedom is a court sentence; that's why freedom is too heavy to bear . . .

Clamence ends by asking for a second chance to save the woman from drowning and thus save himself, but he knows that it is too late.

Camus in these works, and perhaps even more clearly in *The Myth of Sisyphus*,[7] is concerned about man's view of the world and of himself. Philosophically these views range from nihilism to self-deception or delusion. Ultimately, the former involves suicide, and the latter, religion or a comparable metaphysic which avoids the reality of worldly existence. Camus concludes that the meaning and worth of life is the most urgent of human questions.

In suicide one confesses that life is not worth the trouble because it has lost meaning or grandeur. The need for suicide implies a feeling of an Absurd[8] world in which the "opposites" can never be reconciled. Camus says:

> . . . in a universe suddenly divested of illusions and lights, man feels an alien, a stranger. His exile is without remedy since he is deprived of the memory of a lost home or the hope of a promised land. This divorce between man and his life, the actor and his setting, is properly the feeling of absurdity. . . . Belief in the absurdity of existence must dictate his conduct.

That the world is never as man wants it, but is as it is in reality, has always been known. The history of man has been the history of successive attempts to ameliorate reality and even today there is no consensus as to how this can best be done. The individual is left to determine his own fate, although there are insti-

[7] New York: Knopf, 1957. These philosophical ideas are also implemented by Camus in *The Plague* (New York: Knopf, 1957), and *The Exile and the Kingdom* (London: Hamish Hamilton, 1958).

[8] Camus uses both an upper- and a lower-case letter *A* for the Absurd. In direct quotations, I follow his usage. In other instances, the capital *A* is used.

tutional processes such as psychoanalysis, religion, and education which offer him help. Man's behavior in the world is then the effort to cope with the feeling of Absurdity which engulfs him: with the finite nature of his being when he would be infinite; with the discrepancy between his intellect and the not so rational social order in which he lives; with his feeling of impotence when he is the most potent of the earth's species. Camus sees this in a relativistic way when he defines the Absurd as:

. . . the comparison between a bare fact and a certain reality, between an action and the world that transcends it. The absurd is essentially a divorce. It lies in neither of the elements compared: it is born of their confrontation. . . . absurd is not in man (if such a metaphor could have a meaning) nor in the world, but in their presence together. For the moment it is the only bond uniting them.

Each man, then, struggles with his Absurd, with his own confrontation of the world, and comes to a conclusion (consciously and unconsciously) regarding his position or stance in it. Camus sums it up in this way:

And carrying this absurd logic to its conclusion, I must admit that the struggle implies a total absence of hope (which has nothing to do with despair), a continual rejection (which must not be confused with renunciation), and a conscious dissatisfaction (which must not be compared to immature unrest). Everything that destroys, conjures away, or exercises these requirements (and, to begin with, consent which overthrows divorce) ruins the absurd and devaluates the attitude that may then be proposed. The absurd has meaning only insofar as it is not agreed to.

Fromm-Reichmann once said, "It is my belief that the problems and emotional difficulties of mental patients, neurotics and psychotics, are in principle rather similar to one another and also to the emotional difficulties in living from which we all suffer at times."[9] My contention in this chapter is that the problem of schizophrenia mirrors the problems of all people, and that it represents one mode of existence among the many that can be chosen. It is one way of eluding the Absurd. The hypothesis of the "doublebind,"[10] if removed from the limiting and situational context in which its authors place it, seems to be the problem of the Absurd in the larger sense. The Absurd is the double-bind par excellence and the model for all others to come.

But if schizophrenia is an elusive reaction to the Absurd, therapists do not know why it manifests itself in this particular way, nor what finally distinguishes the schizophrenic from the neurotic who also reacts defensively to the Absurd. The therapist is forced to posit special predispositions to such behavior. After years of study, Fromm-Reichmann came to the almost simplistic conclusion that schizophrenics were predisposed to require more love than other people.[11] I believe it may also be possible that there are people sensitized to the Absurd who can neither commit suicide nor embrace a faith which permits them to deny its reality. Nothing is left to them but to withdraw from the game of life and become semi-nonparticipants. In my observation, chronic schizophrenics rarely commit suicide, nor are they particularly distinguished by their religious feelings or affiliations. Camus' characters Meursault and Clamence are thus schizophrenic, or schizophrenic-like, because they do not approach the question of the Absurd with direct confrontation, but with an aloof and splitting evasion that is compromising to the psyche.

Whether or not a person is diagnosed as schizophrenic is not always a function of his autochthonous state. Recent evidence indicates that such a diagnosis may be a function of culture, and of the

[9] Fromm-Reichmann, Frieda. *Principles of Intensive Psychotherapy.* Chicago: University of Chicago Press, 1950, p. xi.

[10] Bateson, G., Jackson, D. D., Haley, J., and Weakland, J. "Toward a Theory of Schizophrenia." *Behavioral Science,* 1956, *1,* 251–264.

[11] Personal communication from Helm Stierlin.

healer as a part of culture.[12] Nor do any two psychiatrists uniformly agree that any single patient is schizophrenic. It is fashionable today to dilute the prognostic significance of the term by modifiers involving such terms as "affective," "psychopathic," and so forth. The understanding of schizophrenia is being generalized away from narrow Kraepelinian confines to account for modern social forces. Society has difficulty tolerating those who cannot cope with the Absurd in a normative fashion. Persons who disturb society's equanimity are segregated, because they threaten society's own balance. Since they cannot be considered criminal, they must be sick and must eventually be placed in hospitals. Thus there is a direct reciprocal relationship between the homeostasis of a culture and the number of its hospitalized schizophrenics.

Camus' solution to the dilemma of existence is neither in the direction of escapist metaphysics nor in the termination of life. It is rather a being-in-the-world with all of its terrible implications and consequences. It is the direct confrontation of the Absurd, and its acceptance as "this is the life to be lived" because there is no other. The horrific burden of continuity in existence, of something after death, has no meaning because the here-now is man's true involvement. Only when life is not currently lived does an afterlife become important. Thus Janine, in *The Exile and the Kingdom*, worn by years of habit and boredom and unfulfilled in marriage, stands on the parapet overlooking the Sahara Desert, speechless, unable to tear herself away from the vast void open before her. "Over yonder, still farther south, at that point where sky and earth meet in a pure line—over yonder it suddenly seemed there was awaiting her something of which though it had always been lacking, she had never been aware of until now."[13] She wants to be liberated even if Marcel, her husband, cannot be free. However, after a desperate inner struggle, Janine goes silently back to her husband's bed to resume her former life and her burden. Raskolni-

[12] Hollingshead, A. B., and Redlich, F. C. *Social Class and Mental Illness: A Community Study*. New York: Wiley, 1958.
[13] *The Exile and the Kingdom*, p. 23.

kov in *Crime and Punishment* goes to the detective, Ilya Petrovitch, to confess his crime although he knows the murders cannot be proved against him. In confronting Petrovitch he falters and leaves the police station wanting to be free. He encounters Sonia, whom he loves, on the steps; he looks at her for a moment and turns back to confess, dooming himself to Siberia, but also to Sonia's enduring love.

The problem of schizophrenia is the problem which Camus poses. It is the problem of an existence which has no inner meaning and value. With schizophrenics it is a matter of psychic life or death. and they feel it is better not to love at all than to love somewhat. These formulations have implications for the psychotherapy of schizophrenia.

It has been pointed out that two principal factors delaying the application of psychotherapy to the schizophrenic are his narcissism, which makes him resist a transference relationship, and his inability to communicate.[14] It is now recognized that these limiting conditions are rooted in the need of the therapist to keep his distance from the schizophrenic.[15] With a more suitable psychodynamic theory, therapists have come to understand the defensive or eluding function of the schizophrenic's narcissism and have stopped expecting him to relate as neurotics do. By developing a willingness to enter the schizophrenic world, therapists have at once cut through supposedly impenetrable barriers.

Emphasis on the curative value of insight has also had repercussions on the psychotherapy of schizophrenia. As long as therapists' criteria of improvement stressed the completeness of the patient's self-knowledge, the importance of the schizophrenic's relationship to his reality was overlooked. Insight is a necessary ingredient for the gratification of the therapist, but it does not necessarily stir the patient to action. Too often the conclusion of a course of

[14] See footnote 1.

[15] Stierlin traces the history of this trend to Aristotelian modes of thought. See "Contrasting Attitudes Toward the Psychoses in Europe and in the United States." *Psychiatry*, 1958, *21*, 141–147.

psychoanalysis or psychotherapy was noted as "Has developed the appropriate insight but is unable to act upon it." The implications of nonverbal communication, inherent in the encounter in terms of icons, symbols, archetypes, and more primitive message units, were completely ignored. Therapists spent many hours dissecting the content and structure of the schizophrenic's thinking while they overlooked him as a human being. Instead of providing a corrective interpersonal experience, they tried to put the fragments of the schizophrenic's mind together again. As Sullivan said, "The greatest harm to patients comes from the conventional situations in which the schizophrenic has rubbed into him more of the worn-out ethics which are intimately related with the eruption of his psychoses." And, again, "Another way of stating this is that with psychotics the attempt is to strengthen the force of logical appreciation of the outside world and bring the normal amount of pressure to bear upon the released unconscious tendencies."[16] Sullivan recognized early that schizophrenia was a specific problem neither of the id nor of the superego, but of the relation of the ego to its reality. He saw the problem rightly as an interpersonal one, both in its genesis and its treatment.

All psychotherapies of schizophrenia today, following their logical conceptual development, stress the "being together" of patient and therapist, and the unique existence of each. Something is "given" back and forth in the interpersonal situation which is called "love," but the giving may have unique and diverse manifestations. The personality of the therapist, with the attendant transference, countertransference, and counteridentification, is an important factor in treatment. Malone explains:[17]

The personality of the therapist, the bilateral process of therapy, and the emotional interchange in the therapeutic experience all assume critical importance in the treatment of schizophrenia . . . the more

[16] Harry Stack Sullivan, quoted in Brill, A. A. "Schizophrenia and Psychotherapy." *American Journal of Psychiatry*, 1929, 9, 518–541.
[17] Whittaker, C. (Ed.). *Psychotherapy of Chronic Schizophrenic Patients*. Boston: Little, Brown, 1958.

fundamental problems of contact and communication loom much larger. The personal relationship of the therapist to the psychotic patient emerges as a vital treatment factor. The intensity of the emotions expressed by the psychotic and the primitiveness of the content of his production and behavior contribute to this emphasis.

My formulation of schizophrenia involves Malone's and Sullivan's concepts but places a greater emphasis and responsibility on the patient for being what he is and for becoming what he wants to be. It recognizes that he has a choice not only of his symptoms but of the place he would like to take in the world. The therapist puts his own ego and reality at the service of the patient in an *encounter* which is a deep and symbolic communion. The therapist does not "give" in the conventional sense of the word. He enters a growth process which challenges his own existence, that is, his control, reality, and unconscious processes. In the past, the most successful psychotherapists of schizophrenia have been women who have been described as saints or saint-like.[18] While it does not require a saint, or even a woman, to treat a chronic schizophrenic, the quality of interaction needed with such a patient resembles the beatification which comes from the exquisite tenderness of mother to wanted infant or from lover to lover.[19]

The encounter differs from classical transference in the sense that two beings are tested by the Absurd in a symbolism of the past, and in the here-now. It is a working out of a common fate at the present moment, but it also includes the drama or tragedy of the past. Each participant bears witness to the suffering and joys

[18] Eissler, K. R. "Remarks on the Psychoanalysis of Schizophrenia." In *Psychotherapy with Schizophrenics,* Brody, E. B., and Redlich, F. C., Eds. New York: International Universities Press, 1952, pp. 130–167.

[19] I cannot conceive of the successful treatment of a chronic schizophrenic without this transcendental quality, that seems to be present in all such relationships. I realize that my analogies here do not describe the inherent nature of this phenomenon. I feel helpless, moreover, in the face of so complex and transfiguring an experience. Possibly in this modern age new devices will be discovered that will permit one to measure such experience directly without resorting to inadequate metaphors.

of the other, and each clarifies the meaning of the Absurd. It then becomes possible to see the Absurd not as a negation of life but as offering a fruition of it. Awareness of the reality of the moment without misconception or delusion is reward enough for existence. As Camus says, "For if there is a sin against life, it consists perhaps not so much in despairing of life as in hoping for another life and in eluding the implacable grandeur of this life."[20] Thus the problem of the schizophrenic comes back to the problem of whether to exist in the face of reality. All else is secondary.

The encounter mirrors the principal transcendental associations of earlier life and encompasses the totality of life and its meaning. It is an identification that is immediate, unique, and lasting. Its structure is largely unconscious. It is the primary meeting of unconscious with unconscious in its most symbolic manifestation and establishes the framework of higher-level "symbolic realization."[21]

Having made the decision to elude life, the schizophrenic cannot be asked to revoke his stance. He cannot be offered promises or rewards which will lead him to give up his narcissism, withdrawal, and fantasies. Guarantees that the world is no longer Absurd cannot be provided. Life offers no guarantees to anyone, and therapists cannot be apostles of apologia. The significant thing is that the patient is led to "meaning" through the therapeutic relationship, through a deep emotional process not as yet completely understood.

The conception of schizophrenia as a form of existence, as a way of eluding an Absurd world, or as alienation from it, poses to the therapist the problem of his own existence and his defensive maneuvers. Few therapists are willing to face, or possibly are capable of facing, their own Absurd existence for the benefit of the patient. To do so puts therapists to the severest test. But no therapy of schizophrenia can endure without the dedication of the therapist

[20] *The Myth of Sisyphus,* p. 162.
[21] The *technique* of the encounter has no influence on its mediation and can vary from the directness of a Rosen to the serenity of a Sechehaye. In either instance all of the elements of the encounter are present.

26

and his personal conviction that in the Absurd there is essential meaning and beauty. This is the therapeutic commitment at its best. All matters of technique in therapy contribute to creating a setting for an enfolding sense of being-in-the-world and the choice the patient may come to make about his fate. The therapist is neither a guide nor a leader. He accompanies the patient in his journey on a number of levels of symbolic involvement. This understanding of the psychotherapeutic relationship in schizophrenia is fundamental and makes possible the application of specific techniques.

# CHAPTER 3

# Schizophrenic Temporality

---

In the psychotherapy of schizophrenic patients distinctions between patient and psychotherapist are sharper and more critical than with neurotics. These distinctions early led to the widely accepted belief that a transference was impossible with a schizophrenic patient. Examination of the differences between patient and therapist have been evaded in the past by the use of diagnostic constructs. I am concerned in this chapter with only one facet of the problem, but one which basically cuts across the relationship between patient and therapist. This is the aspect of *time*, or temporality.

Time is a subtle, enveloping concept which serves culture well. It may, in fact, be the clearest single mark of acculturation, and it certainly occupies a central position in the dilemma of modern man, in the human condition. To be time-bound is to be culture-bound. Recently, psychology and psychiatry have been concerned with the duration of psychotherapy, and have sought ways of reducing its length. Thus we have group therapy, family therapy, transactional analysis marathon therapy, psychodrama, and even brief therapy which takes only one hour or two—all designed to speed things up. Not much thought, however, has been given to the meaning of time within the therapeutic setting itself or to its dynamic meaning to the individual participants. It is becoming apparent that schizophrenia may be a variant form of existence and, as such, may be a part and product of culture, a product, however, with specific psychopathological connotations. It may well be that the experience of time is in some way related to schizophrenia, and that a new perspective about temporality may assist in closing the gap between patient and therapist and in this way help the cure.

Time has no meaning and no content of its own. It is a universal fluid which provides coherency to process. We have reified time and by so doing surrendered qualia for quantum.[1] Shlien poses the problem in this way:[2]

Time is an abstract concept having no concrete or active properties of its own, and therefore practically means nothing. We all realize that time is measured only by change, but life in a clock culture wrongly teaches us to think otherwise. We learn to think in terms of a "9 to 5" work day, not of work. The legal code tells us that time "is of the essence." It is not. The true essence is energy. We are told, in the psychological realm, that "time heals." It does not. All the time in the world cannot heal anything. There is some healing process, which we barely know, taking place in time. Merely "putting in time" signifies nothing, leads to nothing.

There is a mythology of time to which all of us cling tenaciously. This myth involves the causality and productivity of time, its infi-

[1] The present emphasis on mathematics and quantification in our culture is directly related to time-boundedness. It is what existential philosophy seeks to counteract. Man's freedom must also be related to *his* perception of time. While mathematics gives us greater precision, it becomes more and more alienated from its subject and, more seriously yet, the scientist himself falls a victim by partialing himself out of the total human scene.

[2] Shlien, J. "What Length and Intensity for Psychotherapy?" Paper presented before the American Psychological Association, Cincinnati, 1959.

29

nite nature, and its regenerative, reliving qualities. Subscription to the myth leads to the belief that one moment is as good as the next, one day like any other, this week like last week. A temporal sameness is produced which becomes the characteristic of man's humdrum existence. He often waits patiently for time to change something in his life, but only comes desperately to his finiteness. Then he may have feelings that if he cannot live forever, he would rather not live at all. Time is a constant, he believes, and relativity a particle on a great Absolute.

The psychotherapist is not immune to temporal myths and time is in fact very troublesome for him. He looks forward to a certain elapsed time in his training and to the end of his training analysis. In his practice he is constantly arranging and disarranging time, and the loss of his appointment book is apt to produce panic. His income and status tend to be measured by therapeutic time; in addition, he is expected to have a spouse, raise children, be a member of the community, and participate in scientific ventures, all in the limited temporal span allotted him. The involvement of the psychotherapist with time is perhaps even greater than that of other professional men. This is not surprising for it is precisely the problem of time, of finiteness and infinity, that the schizophrenic and other patients bring to him, and the psychotherapist is himself involved with the problem of his own finite existence.[3] While these problems may be recognized by him, their exact contribution to the treatment of the schizophrenic patient is frequently overlooked.

If two people meet for therapeutic purposes, and the value-system of one is time-bound and the other timeless, the result, on both sides, is a feeling of frustration. Time, like space, is a fundamental of being-in-the-world; if there is no agreement on the basic parameter on which the human drama is played, then it is easy to

---

[3] It is easy for the psychotherapist to believe that he goes on and on. There are plausible reasons he can give to convince himself. It therefore comes as a considerable shock to psychotherapists when a prominent psychoanalyst dies. Such feelings lend confirmation to our own involvement with time in a special way.

see that the schizophrenic patient will be loath to resolve the human dilemma of the Absurd. For the schizophrenic, the fifty-minute hour or twice-a-week visit is meaningless. He does not understand the artificialities which surround the fifty-minute hour. Everything for him is archaic, paleologic, and symbolic. It is exactly because time has lost its meaning that the patient is in therapy. Most men are very much aware of their chronological age and of the physical alterations in them which indicate the passing of time. However, if a schizophrenic patient is asked his age, he will in good faith say at one time that he is twenty, and at another forty. The matter of time is just not relevant in the schizophrenic situation.

There are then, in a necessary sense, two parallel time-systems, the patient's and the psychotherapist's, which must be reconciled. This reconciliation cannot be taken lightly, for experience indicates that most psychotherapists cannot accomplish it, and that it comes only with the greatest difficulty. The psychotherapist is not privileged;[4] he is merely a being encountering another being, and one cannot say whose time will apply.

There are a number of problems the temporal situation poses, but I will consider only one. We say that the schizophrenic patient develops a thinking disorder which is paleologic in nature and that it lacks communicative properties. We can demonstrate his neologisms on vocabulary or association tests and they seem to deviate from what we know of as logical thinking. We can then use such deviations themselves as diagnostic hallmarks of schizophrenia. Consider for a moment a simple statement made by a schizophrenic after hours of apparently fruitless psychotherapy: "Let us try one another."[5] This remark has the cryptic, symbolic, and paleologic import of all schizophrenic thinking. What it does is to communicate something of the greatest moment in an iconographic and alienated way. The patient is saying to her psychotherapist: "I find

---

[4] I have borrowed this phrase from Jean-Paul Sartre. *Existential Psychoanalysis*. New York: Philosophical Library, 1953.

[5] This was reported to me by Harold Searles. The interpretation is mine.

31

you worthy as a human being and I entrust my being to you. While I am content to leave this Absurd world behind, you have revived my faith in it and I will meet you in all my humanity." Another schizophrenic hospitalized for a long period in a state hospital says, "I am not worthy of being a resident in this hospital." Yet she knows that she has come to the end of the road, having failed to recover after several years of treatment in a university hospital, and that she may be hospitalized for the remainder of her life. What does she mean by her statement? Is it that in her eyes she has become so degraded that she is not worthy of the company of fellow patients, or of her therapist? Does it not tell us of the condition of her being-in-the-world in a unique and significant way? What is meant by the patient who says, "My mother is holding my feelings in trust for me"?

There is actually no such thing as schizophrenic thinking. There is only paradoxical and metaphoric thinking adapted in its logical and communicative properties to one's world as one experiences it. Since time is not intrinsic, the schizophrenic cannot abide by the logical and cultural aspects of temporal thought and cuts across them by abridgement and symbolization. This gives schizophrenic thinking its peculiar property.

Time involves the problem of the moment, the past, and of infinity. I am principally involved here with the former. In everyday life, the moment is considered to be without special substance, of a highly transitory nature, and of little consequence. Every moment is like all other moments and transitivity applies. When we ask a friend to wait a moment, we actually mean several moments, and the significance of that special moment is thus lost. It is reasonable to behave in this way if one believes that there is an infinity of future transitive moments, or that the past governs without regard to the present. Despite the discreditation of the moment, we all know that we have experienced a number of critical and peak moments in our lives that have determined our fate. These may have occurred with or without conscious participation, but we were aware that they were of the greatest significance. Incredulousness may actually be a defense against the moments of birth, saying "I do" (in marriage), conception, career commitment, which bind "forever and ever." We are familiar with those moments in which fate and destiny side.

We like to assume that time has certain unique properties that serve our needs. If it were simply a matter of sidereal or mathematical time, the problem would be simplified. We would have exact physical units of time capable of being set into a framework of relativity theory. We anchor the time, so to speak, to some higher and natural order of regularity, and even though we do not understand the nature of the regularity, it governs the time which is inner to man. We then proceed to differentiate and segment our lives on this basis. Unfortunately, all men do not participate in such a physical process with their being. They are caught up in it as prisoners, and despair of it. Their inner or psychological time is not of this order, and it is their inner nature that is attempting reconciliation. Several experiments of mine demonstrated that a time interval varies according to whether one feels bored or motivated, engaged or disengaged, as well as with the nature of the event occurring in time.[6] If the average man is forced to depend only on psychic-time, his response will be anxiety. If the deprivation is sufficiently long and intense, psychotic-like behavior may follow.

Thus, a moment is not like all other moments. It is a moment-for-itself and must be understood this way. Of course, moments do elide into themselves and become sequential moments or processes. The moment can be considered an existential referent to self being at a place or location of significance. It is the medium through which life and existence are translated, but it has no intrinsic value in its own right. Without some such intellectual formulation, however, time could not be used as currency. With schizophrenics

[6] "Relation of Time Estimation to Satiation." *Journal of Experimental Psychology*, 1939, *25*, 281–293. "A Further Study of the Relation of Time Estimation to Monotony." *Journal of Applied Psychology*, 1943, *27*, 350–359. "Behavioral Characteristics of Monotony in Two Age Groups." *Journal of Experimental Psychology*, 1943, *33*, 332–339.

the moment is of the greatest significance; in a sense, it is the secret of his existence. He is in despair because psychic-time stands still while all about him moves. The future is unreachable because there is no present, so he attempts to be as before. His personal negation is the negation of the principal hallmark of culture: time. He cannot and refuses to live by time as we know it, and there is no greater rebellion in the eyes of culture. Nations in such a timeless condition are regarded as backward, while we are apt to call such individuals sick.

The schizophrenic's perversion of time is followed by the alteration of space. To occupy the minimum of time, the schizophrenic employs the smallest of space: he does not move. The temporal-spatial disorder thus fixes him once and for all on a sickness continuum to which we then give a distinctive clinical cognomen. Persons in such a state are excruciatingly aware of the significance of the moment. They seek and evade the critical moment—so that soon all moments become critical and none are critical. They live in a kind of watchful, social anarchy in which moments affirm and disaffirm in an excruciating way.

The schizophrenic patient's waking life is analogous to dreaming. The dream is not governed by the temporal-spatial circumstances of the waking life. It gets right to the "heart of the matter" without regard for the perceptual niceties the ego is accustomed to. Eons become moments and moments eons. Displacements and substitutions occur. History returns with a presence heretofore unknown.

The therapeutic encounter with the psychotherapist becomes a vehicle for the moment and its meaning. Above all, the psychotherapist represents the unconscious part of the schizophrenic's conscious. He is the medium through which the thesis of the unconscious is synthesized with the antithesis of the conscious. The psychotherapist becomes the patient's Other; he is himself, but he is also a significant unknown part of the patient. Such a process is not only to be understood by introjection or identification; it is a present-and-past relationship symbiotically rooted in the history of all mankind. The psychotherapist has, like the layman, tended to ignore the significance of the moment in place of capturing it. He seeks a breakthrough in content-complex rather than in time-complex. He clutches at time-oriented existence and is frightened by the schizophrenic's boundless temporal referent. He cannot see the moment-for-itself in terms of immediate experience with the patient. In his hypothesis-making "preludium to interpretation" he organizes the patient's time world into his own and thus tends to deny the encounter between them.

The example of the bullfight offers a parallel to the therapeutic process. In Spain the bullfight is of tremendous personal and collective significance.[7] It is not just a sport like, let us say, soccer. The bullfighter and his role signify the game of life and death for the Spaniard who must continually renew or affirm himself. In the bull ring a man faces, against great odds, a bull specifically bred for his destruction. There is no pretense in the ring, and the crowd will brook no displacements, sublimations, or other defenses. It is kill or be killed. The most sensitive and momentous part of this process is the *moment of truth:* either the bull is killed with one thrust of the sword, or the matador is gored. It is the moment in which man faces his greater reality, his instincts, his being alone, and he must measure up. If he does, there is no greater acclaim and no greater feeling of self-esteem. The spectator is a deep participant in the process. In Spain, where life for the average man is still hard, the moment of truth symbolizes man's humanity and purpose in the face of a Nature which often fails to distinguish between its species.

The schizophrenic, too, has his moment of truth. This moment is apt to come with his psychotherapist at the turning points in treatment. It occurs when the schizophrenic accepts the Absurd as his burden, and continues in a culture that is often paradoxical and meaningless. This acceptance takes place when he encounters his psychotherapist as a fellow human being in the full disclosure of person to person and is able to give and receive intimacy. It is

[7] This was true at the time this was written. Today the corrida is beginning to lose its dynamic.

then, at his moment of truth, that he makes his own existential choice. The problem of the moment is an old one philosophically, but it has relevance to what we try to do in psychotherapy. It explains why, for example, psychotherapists are so preoccupied with the beginnings and endings of psychotherapy,[8] and why they bog down in these phases more than in any others.

To enter and to exit are existentially problems of the same order as to be. These problems are of interest here because they relate to the psychic time of the schizophrenic patient and psychotherapist. To enter is to accept a burden for which the gratification may fail to compensate. To be committed to a project (in Sartre's terms) is both confining and transcending. Such commitments, however, do not come easily. An ultimate reference of entry is the commitment of birth. It is common for schizophrenic patients to wish they had not been born. The original commitment of birth was both an insult and an opportunity, but it cannot obliterate the symbolic wish for noncommitment.

In the psychotherapy of schizophrenia the entry is a most important project. Each participant enters the life of the other through a basic commitment of considerable scope that parallels the greatest moments in one's being. The entry with the schizophrenic patient is usually made quickly and momentarily, although it is buttressed by many special but extraneous considerations. One knows rather quickly, however, whether one wants to treat this patient. Temporally, the commitment is enduring. All considerations of time are abstract and only for the convenience of the psychotherapist. There is no beginning as such, for somewhere in the past the patient has encountered the psychotherapist-prototype; otherwise, transference would be impossible. The patient then enters

---

[8] My analysis of the addendum responses to case histories of treatment for a broad cross-section of psychoanalysts and psychotherapists reveals that selecting patients for such treatment, and terminating them once the process has come to a conclusion, is a difficult thing. The practices are quite diverse. See Burton, A. (Ed.). *Case Studies in Counseling and Psychotherapy*. Englewood Cliffs: Prentice-Hall, 1959.

something already historically true and interprets it as such. (This is why schizophrenic patients are always wondering where they have met you before.) The patient wants only to assure himself that it really is a continuation, and that there will not be the abrupt exit that occurred previously.

These temporal conceptions of psychotherapy are of the greatest dynamic significance for the treatment. They allow entry of one to the other in the only temporality possible to the patient. They place the stress on the you-and-I-together-in-the-world rather than on mediative properties that are necessarily obstructive, because artificial. They allow the psychotherapist to draw on his own humanity in the relationship rather than on technical maneuvers oriented toward content, and to see the patient as a life in process in a world of the patient's making.

Schizophrenic patients have a "slimy" quality in that they stick fast to what they have. Disengagement is difficult and schizophrenics tend to choke off with their "slime." This is frightening to the psychotherapist and poses the problem of eventual exit. My thesis is that there is no exit, that only as the patient entered will he exit. His relationship to the psychotherapist is everlasting but symbolized. Just as a man never really gives up the symbol of his mother, the schizophrenic patient similarly does not yield the treasure he has found in his rare and wondrous encounter with the therapist. Exit is, of course, related to the final one which sets the anxiety pattern for all exit facsimiles. With the schizophrenic patient this is much more critical, since he has already symbolically exited but has not had the courage for the final step that is physical death. For him, reentry means no exit, and he seeks an enduring relationship with his psychotherapist. Under these circumstances, time-limited psychotherapy with a schizophrenic patient is a misnomer.

The philosophical aspects of temporality presented here as they are related to the treatment of the schizophrenic patient may present practical difficulties. Many patients have to be seen, and the psychotherapist is faced not only with earning a livelihood but with a proper use of his time. With this I agree. However, it must be noted that even an attitudinal change about temporality in the psychotherapist is elevating, so that the relationship is already different and the treatment need not continue forever. Those who treat schizophrenics therapeutically are a select group by their dedication and, if the personal values that make this dedication possible are meaningful, then growth in temporality must also be accepted as a desideratum.

We must become aware of the significance of certain moments in treatment and be capable of experiencing them as well as interpreting them. In the history of man, momentary conversion experiences have often been decisive for a man's history. Something analogous could be true for the schizophrenic patient. The psychotherapy is not necessarily a conversion experience, but moments-of-being-in-the-world-with-the-psychotherapist might be crucial in determining the patient's future choices. It may be possible that the often routine and lengthy path of psychotherapy can be shortened by a better appreciation of the way points in their fuller temporal meaning.

# CHAPTER 4

# Loneliness as Schizophrenia

---

Loneliness[1] is a universal human phenomenon and is to be considered not only in its pathological aspects but for its meaning for the human condition. In schizophrenia the problem of loneliness is so intense and so central as to serve as a special laboratory for the understanding of its phenomenology. It is through the psychotherapy of the schizophrenic patient that we have arrived at insights about loneliness that may possibly have significance for all men.

If we assume that life is a unity, then being-in-the-world is

---

[1] By loneliness I mean not the secondary loneliness that comes with the loss of a human or human-like object, but rather the essential loneliness which is a part of the primary process and in which the individual becomes separated from his inner world and its referents. Henry von Witzleben distinguishes these as primary and secondary loneliness. (See "On Loneliness." *Psychiatry*, 1958, *21*, 37–43). Frieda Fromm-Reichmann calls it *real* loneliness (See Bullard, D. M. (Ed.). *Psychoanalysis and Psychotherapy: Selected Papers of Frieda Fromm-Reichmann*. Chicago: University of Chicago Press, 1959, pp. 325–336).

a part of that unity. The individual requires historicity, presence, and becoming, in a cosmic setting as the totality of his continuity, and without it he feels fragmented. A person has boundaries: his skin, and another of a more psychic kind. He has a deep need to flow beyond these boundaries toward the total physical and psychological world, and in this way feel at one with nature. If he cannot do this, he is left with the thought of being cut off, of alienation, and loneliness is the feeling response. He speaks of a lack of "meaning" in his life and his need of new values and activities. Obviously, for the infant it is the mothering person who provides the whole. But wholes are dynamic, and, as the child grows, they become ever larger and more complex so that the mother can no longer suffice. The essential holistic system, however, is based on the world of nature, which is the original whole. Since all cultures limit and circumscribe nature, an element of estrangement is produced in every man's life.

There is in each man the dualism I call the Dialogue: the thesis and antithesis by which men maintain the personal boundaries needed to be complete within themselves, but also go beyond themselves to some entity which exists outside. This latter we may say is the archetypal Other.

Loneliness is a need and not a condition. It is the thesis of the Dialogue without which object relations or communication between people becomes impossible. Loneliness is an acute affirmation or proof of existence, and is not a distinction given to all people. Just as it is not possible for everyone to be schizophrenic, so is this acute form of loneliness limited to the relatively few. It is one basis of artistic creation. It affirms by the urgency of feeling and suffering alone the nature of being human. Nevertheless, we seek desperately to dispel loneliness in the most frenetic of ways and hunt for divertissement as a refuge for loneliness. The Dialogue is life's balance between the self and the Other—now it is the self, and now the Other. This is the exquisite play which dynamically makes possible all social relationships. It defines what man is for himself and what the Other is. The escape into activity thus becomes the escape from

40

self. To be lonely is to be dependent on no one. It is to stand alone in the face of one's humanness, one's meaning and purpose, and to meet reality directly. In this way one comes to know oneself and the basic Dialogue becomes possible.

There is in each man the need to transcend himself, to go beyond the needs of his nature: a need for sublimity or ecstasy. It is only through such transcendence that man experiences his full being. In ecstasy, all of the social bonds that confine man are removed, and there is a soaring that unifies inner and outer identities. The transcending moments set the design for the "possible"; they exemplify a longing for what might be, compared to what is. The felt discrepancy between what is and what might be is the hallmark of one's state of being-in-the-world. The larger the discrepancy, the greater the feeling of loneliness. Loneliness is not a problem for ecstatic psychotics, since they have permitted their inner identity to overflow in a way known only to the primary process: What is *is* what might be. To find ecstasy is, however, the most difficult thing in the world unless one can be psychotic. I suspect that the search for ecstasy is in part the reason for the millions of gallons of alcoholic beverages consumed each year as well as the various psychedelic medicaments which temper the nervous system. Unfortunately, ecstasy cannot be cheaply purchased. Those who have a lower threshold for it, that is, need to be constantly sustained by it, are vulnerable to a pathological loneliness. Indeed, loneliness can itself become a form of ecstasy. In schizophrenic patients loneliness and ecstasy are to be seen in a unique combination. The need to be ecstatic, to be more than what mundane life has made possible, is the characteristic need of the schizophrenic patient. What for some is a meaningful form of existence may become for the schizophrenic a confused Absurd with no reconciliation possible.

If one is not what one is, and one's primary need is for a transcendent ecstasy, one becomes lonely when one is cut off from the greater whole which is uniquely experienced. Loneliness then becomes the sign of existence and one becomes obsessed with the acuteness of life. Community is with the other lonely ones and cate-

41

gories of "insider" and "outsider" are psychically created. This adds to the sense of estrangement, for the "outsiders" remain practically outside, and the congregation does not work. Perfection is the royal road to becoming ecstatic, but no mortal can be perfect. The unattainable goal and logic of perfection, however, does not reduce the search. At any rate, it is certainly not the perfection of the neurotic which the schizophrenic patient seeks. The neurotic finds perfection in impulse. The schizophrenic wants it in the form of a higher order of meaning even beyond that which the mothering person was originally capable of furnishing him. (He was at times also lonely with her.) She was the prototype of his world, but his inner identity demanded an even deeper and more universally symbolic meaning of existence of which she herself was merely a sign. Thus he begins the secret search for a Nirvana that is to be everlastingly denied him.

Ecstasy as a goal in itself can only lead to pathological loneliness and alienation. Man's purpose in life is not to be ecstatic, but to be himself within a social order of things. The real world is a burden which must be faced and accepted, yet, as Camus has shown, this need not rule out an inner transcendent identity. We need to know why it is so difficult for the schizophrenic person to compromise his existential aims, aims which seem to come easier for other people, or are at any rate less inclusive. For an individual to be complete, to be his authentic self, he must feel related to his total world. He must have a sense of meaning and continuity in nature. He seeks such relatedness in moments of ecstatic experience which unify him and which, because of their rarity and transcendence value, become the object of the search for perfection. When he is cut off from this he feels unloved or alienated.

Western man has reacted to his loneliness by a great spurt of group behavior and by an obsessive interest in group dynamics. Industry and business have become group centered,[2] and therapy in the multifarious, group form is threatening the classic dyadic

[2] A countervailing tendency toward individual decision is now becoming apparent.

variety. Despite this tremendous recent increase in "groupiness," the feelings of loneliness have kept pace with group growth and even outdistanced it. It was Jung who pointed out that, particularly in the United States, the child is deprived of the solitude necessary to find himself. The schedule his mother arranges for him keeps him going from one group to another without letup. This must be compensatory for the loss of integration of the family, and the group flight of the mothering person herself. We act as if we believe that to be alone were in some way to be contaminated. To look for the solution to loneliness in numbers of contacts is, however, an illusion we can ill afford.

Loneliness is a function of consciousness, and the more sensitive the conscious function, the more poignant the feelings of loneliness. It is questionable whether infrahuman organisms feel lonely. Alienation is an act of human divorcement and loneliness its conscious component. Loneliness brings horror but it has its rewards. Not only is it affirming, but it allows the self the denial of the human burden together with persistence in the human race. It is not easy for a fully acculturated person to know just what this statement means, and to know the sense of freedom as well as the pain it entails.

It is not enough simply to strike loneliness from the mind, or to place the lonely one in a group. He must be able to avail himself of what he finds in the group. What he needs to find is the sense of completeness; he needs to become authentic, and he knows that this can only be done through the Other. There is no more suitable linguistic conception of this process than the word "love" in its broader context. It is love he seeks, perfect, ecstatic, and transcending, and he also seeks identity in love. It is indeed the principal antidote to loneliness, for in the mother/child, father/son, lover/lover, apostle/deity relationship is to be found the prototype of authentication. But men do not pursue the eternal quest of being "the perfect lover" for the repetitive momentary titillation of the orgasm. It is the archaic and contemporary unity of self and the Other, that is, interpersonal relationships of big and little moment, that they

43

want. Its artistic manifestation is poetic love framed by the sensuality of the body. Thus, in the dualism of life, loneliness itself is the thesis and group identity the antithesis. However, the individual always lives in his own right and not for the group. His emergence is narcissistic and is directed towards self-completion. There is no altruism qua altruism.

As I said earlier, the problem of loneliness and alienation is central to schizophrenia. I have yet to see a schizophrenic patient who did not complain of loneliness. It might be said that the schizophrenic patient need not be lonely if only he give up his narcissistic withdrawal, in other words, his schizophrenia. I would rather put it another way. The patient's loneliness precedes his schizophrenia rather than follows it. It is what logically forces him to the special and complex state we call schizophrenia. Schizophrenia today is a rapidly growing syndrome whose virulence and phenomenology is changing form. Were Kraepelin alive now, he would be hard put to identity those forms of schizophrenia to which we apply the descriptive modifiers "pseudo-neurotic," "borderline," "ambulatory." He would disapprove of such hybrid diagnoses as schizo-affective and schizophrenic-psychopath. What has occurred is that schizophrenia is moving away from a medical model to a social model which is more descriptive. We now carefully scrutinize the "field" forces in which the schizophrenic person is enmeshed: his family,[3] his peers, and his wider culture. Freud was indirectly able to show that the repressive culture of his time was conducive to the development of hysteria, a relatively rare disease today.

In Chapter Two, employing some of the philosophical observations of Albert Camus, I postulated that schizophrenia was both a conscious and an unconscious reaction to a life which could not be lived because of its psychological absurdities; that schizophrenia could be theoretically meaningful if it could be seen as a special problem in existence; and that psychotherapy could assist

[3] Jackson, D. D. "The Monad, the Dyad and Family Therapy of Schizophrenia." In Burton, A. (Ed.), *Psychotherapy of the Psychoses*. New York: Basic Books, 1960.

in reversing a process which seemed organically fixed. That contemporary man interprets his life as Absurd has been well portrayed not only by Camus, but by such writers as Kafka, Dostoevski, and Sartre. Observation of the human condition shows that everywhere men seek "meaning" and that schizophrenia increases apace. We must accept that, at least for the considerable majority of people, contemporary life is found wanting. The preoccupation with the female breast in Western culture is the symbolic need of man to offer succor and the need to receive it. But the female breast has become a contemporary symbol of desiccation: Western women enjoy having large breasts, display them, and even enhance them by prostheses, but they do not want them suckled or bitten—necessary functions in human social endeavors.

It is thus necessary for men to rebel against their fate, each in his own fashion. With the schizophrenic patient the rebellion takes a form and intensity heretofore unknown. He simply gives up the "game" of life, or, rather, he plays at a new game, and develops his own fantastic satisfactions. He is not at all prepared to compromise or sublimate as is the rest of humanity, and is thus both a coward and a special form of hero. He cannot successfully follow the artist and express his rebellion in a graphic metaphor, so he is left to his own devices. He becomes his own "island," with his own idiosyncratic logistics and communication. However, if there is one thing society cannot countenance it is people who reject its culture and ways. It controls its aggressive dissidents by a variety of institutional devices but it is somewhat at a loss with those who persistently retreat into passivity. Puzzling behavior such as this, which does not respond to formal societal stricture and punishment, becomes classified as illness and relegated to still other forms of social control in the hospital.

When a schizophrenic patient is taken into psychotherapy, we make implicit promises about the future even though, by training, we verbally disavow promises. We offer communion with the psychotherapist and, through him, an altered world. But we cannot imply a better world for the world is as it is. We cannot even suggest to the patient that he change for he has no conception of the manifold social forms possible and no way to choose among them. The only thing the therapist can do is to accompany the patient on his journey as a participant-observer and provide a bridge across the chasm of social existence—an imperfect bridge, to be sure, but nevertheless one that eventually may be acceptable to him. We do not cure anyone as such, for there is actually nothing to cure. We offer our own authentic self as an ally, in terms of our own loneliness and suffering. Not only do we put our ego at the disposal of the patient, but also our unconscious in all of its creative function. The meaning in life which is our own personal reconciliation with the Absurd becomes a model in the dispersal of the patient's nihilism. For this reason it is the man and not the technique that counts with schizophrenic patients.

For the therapist to rush in and give first aid for loneliness is to miss the point. But this is just what happens, for it is the non-alienated above all who fear alienation. What I would suggest instead is that the therapist attempt to understand and share the patient's being, thereby making it possible for him ultimately to find his verification in something other than loneliness. Unfortunately, the process is long and complex and there are no substitutes.

Loneliness is the need for authentication, for meaning and unity, in a dehumanizing culture, and the confirmation of the psychic aliveness of the individual. Loneliness in its various forms permits the establishment of the self so that the relationship with the Other becomes possible. Without it, the self is deprived and cannot relate to the totality of the world and find its continuity. It becomes estranged. Loneliness is more than the perpetual search for the mothering person who was available in infancy. It is the search for a primordial unity in the archaic past. In this sense Frieda Fromm-Reichmann did not go far enough in her formulation of loneliness. In the schizophrenic patient we find loneliness in its most acute form. Its treatment does not involve treating loneliness as such, but demands an intense therapeutic encounter in which the fundamentals and meaning of existence are tested and revised.

PART **II**

---

# SOME TECHNIQUES OF TREATMENT

CHAPTER 5

# The Meaning of Transference

The limitations of the classical conception of transference as the central fulcrum of all psychotherapy need to be recognized.[1] Not all of the interaction which occurs in psychotherapy is transference and there are extra-transferential aspects of psychotherapy which are usually ignored. Some of these aspects are that the patient needs to exchange his feelings of "badness" or "goodness"; that he seeks a symbolic Other in psychotherapy in a way for which transference does not account completely; and that the "life force" or life-mood component of the psychotherapist is a factor in the outcome of the treatment. All of these conceptions bear upon the understanding of the patient and his way of being-in-the-therapy. They lead to sev-

---

[1] I admire Leo Stone's attempt to temper Freud's strictures on the transference and its analysis, but his position is one of accommodation rather than the reformation which seems the need today. See Stone, L. *The Psychoanalytic Situation. An Examination of its Development and Esential Nature,* New York: International Universities Press, 1961.

49

eral new and provisional postulations that help to clarify what the transference is as we experience it.

In order to be constructive about psychotherapy it is first necessary to be delimiting. This delimitation is the paradoxical state of psychotherapy today. Thus, for example, psychotherapy is above all considered to be a rational process, but observation reveals that it is often more irrational than rational. Again, there is no one personality which can be called the healer personality, and successful psychotherapists have varied from the benignness and saintliness of Marguerite Sechehaye and Gertrude Schwing to the aggressiveness and directiveness of Frederick Thorne and John Rosen. There is no univocal agreement as to who can be a psychotherapist, and there is no single set of training principles which produces a psychotherapist. Similarly, training is not the function of any single scientific or learned discipline. No psychopathological syndrome, or set of syndromes, responds regularly and uniformly to any one psychotherapeutic technique. No one theory of psychogenesis encompasses all of the varied forms of mental illness, and all of the theories do not necessarily explain any single form of mental illness. There is no consensual agreement as to what is and what is not therapeutic, and no agreement as to what specific technique is to be applied at any specific moment to what patient. Finally, there is no reliable and valid way to evaluate the outcome of a psychotherapy.

The confused mixture of optimism and pessimism of psychotherapists themselves regarding what they do is in my opinion due to a confounding of the experimental and clinical in its various manifestations. We operate on a clinical level and expect validation on the empirical, and this applies to the behavioristic therapies as well. We have been trained as empiricists and serve the public as artists. But the artist has the advantage since he is trained in artistry, expresses himself artistically, and evaluates his product in the same way. Diversity in psychotherapy points up the very real possibility that psychotherapy may be an individualized or group process which can never be formulated in the way desired by the behaviorists. It can be denied but not yet rationalized. It has its

50

own peculiar justification, as do all critical human relationships, in the beingness of the participants, and the phenomenology of the therapeutic situation waits upon the phenomenology of the person.

Recently, a subtle change in the way the psychotherapist handles himself in the therapeutic situation has been taking place. The therapist seems to have become much less concerned with what happened to his patient in the pregenital period than he is with the intercurrent situation, that is, with the patient's interpersonal response to the psychotherapy itself, and to the persons in his world. This is not to say that he no longer believes in the classical doctrines of the genesis of psychic conflict, but rather that the therapeutic procedures which logically follow such doctrines are inadequate. Many patients come to have a pretty thoroughgoing fund of information about the origins or causes of their anxious and conflicted feelings, but they often retain their socially disabling symptoms, or shift to something only slightly less debilitating. The last fifty years of therapeutic psychiatry have, I think, made a fetish of the deep personal history of the patient which has resulted in often giving lip service to the patient's livingness situation and the becoming aspects of his life. Freud's startling cures of supposedly unremitting hysterias led us to seek a similar traumatic experience in every patient and to reify insight as curative.

Unfortunately, the kinds of problems which come to the consulting room today are not so conceptually simple as the hysterias. I have sometimes hoped that one or two of my clients would have a hysterical disorder rather than a disorder of alienation. The psychotherapist today is besieged by patients searching for value and meaning and suffering from ennui, gluttony, vague pain, loneliness, and alienation. The problem posed by Freud's patients was essentially how to use the pleasure principle without crippling repression, anxiety, and guilt. Today the problem is how to find standards and meanings in a superabundance of pleasure, and sometimes the therapeutic problem is to provide a modicum of repression and anxiety. The therapist who starts on the traditional quest for the pregenital referents to such need for standards and meaning is often left only with the orifices, for infantile repressions are only part of the human story. There is also the interpersonal world of the moment and the promise of the future. Such projection is not necessarily to be thought of as teleological, for all men look forward with expectation and their expectations influence their present conduct.

If the present and future influence behavior more than we have known, transference and countertransference are insufficient therapeutic formulations in themselves. I have always believed they lacked sufficient breadth and scope as parameters for a most complex relationship phenomenon. I am convinced that not all of the psychotherapeutic relationship is a transference neurosis, and not all of the feelings of the therapist are countertransference. I have even wondered at times whether a transference neurosis as such was at all requisite for the treatment of neurosis.

There is thus a part of the psychotherapeutic situation which is not historical and which is not transference. That is, the reaction of the patient to the psychotherapist, and vice versa, is *for itself* and may have no reference to figures in the past. To say that transference phenomena constitute the only meaningful aspects of the relationship in psychotherapy is to say that any two people in society can have a significant human encounter only because one always is for the other a surrogate from the past. This may in a sense be true, but it is socially unprofitable to conduct human and professional affairs on this basis. Some of the most transcending of human relationships, and particularly those in which intimacy plays a part, have immediacy and presence and their effects are not necessarily altered by an analytic attitude or analytic applications. They are what they are by virtue of the meeting of two people significant to each other in an immediate and future time reference; the symbolism of the past remains merely the past. This is not to rule out transference effects but to put them into their proper perspective.

Such a point of view leads to the conception of psychic illness as a style of life, or a way of being-in-the-world, which no longer serves its bearer. Psychotherapy then not only involves the discovery and release of repressive ideation and conflict, but the inculcation of a new style of life or way of being-in-the-world. This, of course, is a very broad goal that is frightening to the psychotherapist who is more comfortable with the segmented person.

I want to describe what goes on in psychotherapy in terms of the Good-Bad Dialogue, the Other, and the Eros Quotient. It must be understood that this represents only a partial formulation of the psychotherapeutic process.

Every person requires self-definition which he finds through the general and specific experiences of man anchored in a certain endowment. Self-definition implies worth, the sense that one has value. In the process of finding worth, the contributions of the wider social milieu, culture and its subaspects, are frequently overlooked. Thus, for example, psychotherapists are apt to assume that their clients are like they are: white, middle-class, urban, Judeo-Christian, literate; and that they share the specific values and ethics which accompany such social stratifications.[2] This assumption has importance because the middle class more than any other seeks universally to define itself and lacks the historical position of either poverty or aristocracy to support definition. It is an interesting fact that neither the greatly impoverished nor the extremely wealthy come in any great numbers for psychotherapy.

Patients question their worth in an intense and prolonged way and attempt once more to become "valuable" through psychotherapy. Western civilization supports the search for worth by providing a "good-bad" parameter upon which to measure oneself, and Christianity constantly judges man, even at birth. It elevates to special status only those it considers "good," and demeans the rest as sinners. From the first day the child is born, the mother sets out to have a "good" child. She is constantly alerted by her own superego, by her peer culture, and by the various social institutions to stamp out tabooed developmental practices for which she feels

---

[2] I had the opportunity of observing several Negro psychotherapists in action and noted with amazement how easily they too fall into this stereotype when they depart from it in many ways and cannot help doing so.

shame, and she makes this a most important mission in raising her child. As the child becomes adult and leaves his mother, he finds to his dismay that far from losing his "judge," he now has to cope with a culture which defines even more strictly the impulses he can and cannot express, and which, furthermore, reinforces its strictures by a variety of formal institutions that include prisons, hospitals, churches, schools. He thus develops a very real sense of being "good" or "bad." I am not certain that I agree with Alan Watts that the cause of all this is the Christian concept of original sin, that is, that we are all bad to begin with. But I am certain that I have never seen a neurotic whose ego was not troubled by a sense of adequacy and inadequacy and who did not feel judged.

My use of such theologically tainted valuative words as "good" and "bad" may be objectionable, and it may seem that I am accepting Mowrer's extreme position regarding the psychopathology of conflict as "sin." However, "good" and "bad" here simply stand for such age-old conceptions as Conscious and Unconscious, Heaven and Earth, Light and Dark, Left and Right, Apollonian and Dionysian, and other similar polarities upon which man is racked in Western civilization. "Good" therefore stands for conscious, rational, heavenly, right, light, and Apollonian, while "bad" symbolizes unconscious, irrational, earthy, left, dark, and Dionysian. The mental work of the person includes a considerable portion of such self-classification; patients in great part become patients because they feel "bad" and need to feel "good." That is, they want to be conscious, rational, pure, and right people on the side of the angels, but are instead full of darkness, left-handedness, and deep, unconscious ungraceful urges. Whereas it was formerly the function of the Church to arbitrate between the "bad" and the "good" aspects of the person, it now falls more and more to the psychotherapist to do this because the Church has lost its indigenous function in the morals of man. The psychotherapist has become the restorer of grace to man although he has eagerly avoided such a role in the past.

I can give an example of how this works by borrowing the

coinage of Bion. Whatever the membership and composition of a therapeutic group, it sooner or later stratifies itself bi-modally, separating those who play the therapist from those who play the patient. (This of course does not obviate a shift of roles or playing both at once.) The role of psychotherapist in the therapeutic group symbolically represents to the patients that he is good (humane), rational (conscious), right (moral), and light (pure), and that he counters the irrational (unconscious), wrong (immoral), and dark (dirty) forces. In part this explains the parataxic distortion with which patients hold their psychotherapists: that they are ever loving, devoted, and gracious. Each patient internally senses "good" and "bad" aspects of himself and needs someone with whom to deposit his intolerable internalized "badness." In group psychotherapy the patient becomes the psychotherapist as a defense against himself but also in order to shift unconsciously the burden of what he cannot assimilate in his personality.

In other words, culture provides a highly paid and sometimes respected person to assume the unassimilable or "bad" parts of humanity for which men feel guilty, anxious, and despairful, and thereby leaves the patient free to assume untainted the idealized image he has been struggling with. Psychotherapy is thus in a sense a purification process in which the psychotherapist temporarily assumes the unreconstructed parts of the patient for his later reconstruction and the patient introjects an illusion of his ever loving psychotherapist. Of course, all of this takes place at an unconscious level and helps to explain why in a countervalent way people generally find something unclean and unwholesome about psychotherapy. It also reveals why practitioners usually have one door by which patients enter and another by which they leave. The frequent occurrence that patients can feel better in one interview, or indeed feel better by merely making an appointment which they cancel, is understandable. Certainly no psychoanalytic change can take place in one hour of therapy. The psychotherapist stands for the nonjudgmental, benevolent Father who accepts, understands, and excuses all. He helps bridge the "bad" aspects to the "good" aspects which in the final analysis results in self-expression, self-acceptance and self-regard in a world of persons. There are very few places in society where the Father can even be again located,[3] and fewer still where the "bad" aspects can be temporarily (but constructively) deposited. Penal institutions usually fail in their function because no penologist accepts the "bad" in a psychotherapeutic sense. They merely punish in one way or another for evil behavior although they attempt to rehabilitate. If Freud was correct in thinking that the ego must constantly cope with the id, then the fate of Western man is a constant coping with "light" and "darkness" and the psychotherapist serves precisely such a quasi-priestly function.

This analysis of the role of the psychotherapist brings us to the subject of the Other. I am reminded of an interview which Peter Sellers, the versatile screen actor, gave to the press some years ago. When asked what kind of a personality he had which permitted him to play so many varying roles to such perfection, he said that he really didn't know—that the persons who actually knew were his viewers. This is actually a profound statement. No man ever really knows himself and only attains such knowledge through an Other. The Other is both the symbolic and bodily complement in nature which even morphology cannot deny and its value for the preservation of the species is unquestionable. In schizophrenics there is an interesting body-image phenomenon which may also apply to people at large. Schizophrenic patients search desperately for what I call the Unified Body. That is, they seek to locate and define the interpersonal, or loving, parts of their bodies and to integrate their diffused body image. In psychotherapy they look to the Other for their body-image model and for long periods of time communicate only through body language. There is in the psychotherapy of such patients a symbolic fusion of the two body images which, should it occur, bodes well for the treatment.

But the supreme function of the Other is being-with. Whatever one's theoretical outlook, being-with is a basic human need.

[3] See, for example, Kafka's parable in *The Castle*.

The psychotherapist provides being-with for a client who has an excruciating need for an Other for any of a number of psychogenetic reasons, most of which are related to the early mother symbiosis. This involves more than Rogers' unconditional positive regard, for it is not a form of regard at all. Rather, one ego is at the disposal of another in a process which Searles has described as adoration and scorn in an exquisite mixture. It contains all of the elements of love and hate and excludes only physical sexuality. It is for many patients not only the reinstatement of the mother symbiosis but the prototype of all past relationships of human beings and, in this sense, it approaches Jung's conception of the archetype. Under certain circumstances the loss of the Other is considered the loss of self and suicide becomes a very real possibility.

When we take a patient into treatment we temporarily offer ourselves for one or another reason as the Other. In my estimation the most successful practitioners are those who have the fewest reservations in this regard. Countertransference has many shades of meaning and a number of manifestations, but its principal hallmark is the resistance to being the Other. Now it is perfectly proper to have such resistances, for it must be admitted that many of our patients are petulant, unlovable, and boring. But if we elect to throw our lot in with them, we cannot deny the full meaning of the mantle of the healer we have assumed and practiced under. The successful resolution of a psychotherapy involves the channeling of the need for the Other to a more appropriate subject. If this important transposition fails, the psychotherapist must assist the patient in understanding the Self-Other relationship on both symbolic and real levels to the point where he can exist with a reasonable but non-neurotic search, possibly for very long periods. I believe that patients in long-term psychoanalytic psychotherapy never really give up their psychotherapists, but rather convert them to symbols which they carry around in their psyche. Where either of the above resolutions becomes impossible, we must consider the real possibility of an unremitting or process psychosis.

I have found that in fundamentals one sooner or later returns to Freud, and so I must in what I call the Eros Quotient. Freud posited Eros and Thanatos as the two great forces in life: Eros the growth-producing and creative aspects of the person; Thanatos the pull toward equilibrium, quietude, and extinction. While I have always had doubts about Freud's formulation of Thanatos as an instinct, its presence as a factor in life is unmistakable. Each man's life is a balance, or rather a quotient, of Eros and Thanatos, that is, the drive toward creation and growth is always subdivided by the pull toward quietude, equilibrium, and extinction. But the quotient varies dynamically from time to time. All of us are familiar with patients who say that they feel dead in life, and more often than not we actually consider them equivalent to being dead. They have low Eros/Thanatos quotients.

My contention is that successful psychotherapists have high Eros/Thanatos quotients; they are authentic in Heidegger's terms. This is not to say that they are erotic, although they may be this too, but that their creative forces far outweigh the quieting ones. It is such aliveness which permits them to see beauty, value, and responsibility where others see only misery, despair, and indolence. They are convinced that the purpose of civilization is man and not the objects of man. For a long time I failed to understand why my engineering patients were so difficult to deal with. Then I realized that Eros for them had been displaced to bridges, missiles, and roads, that is, to a non-human environment. Once such displacement fails them as a mode of existence they are indeed in dire straits, for they have no basis upon which to relate to man. It is the high Eros/Thanatos quotient which permits a psychotherapist to start treatment with a regressed schizophrenic patient when the literature counsels against it, or to stand unperturbed against the severe onslaughts of the paranoid or obsessed client, or not to give up hope after years of apparent lack of movement with treatment.

The psychotherapist must be fundamentally convinced that the conscious and unconscious both have a place, that the "bad" is a part of the "good," and that the primary process is not to be feared. He constantly reaffirms the livability of life and thus puts in a proper perspective not only his patients' suffering but his own. He does not stop with merely analyzing the transference but offers a positive existential model in the authenticity of his own self.

Psychotherapy is helpful when it is given by an authentic person who has no reservations whatsoever to becoming the Other and who is willing, at least temporarily, to assume the patient's burden of darkness, irrationality, and Dionysian impulse. He encounters his patient, a human being, on both symbolic and realistic levels at the present moment, in the past, and in the "becoming" of the remainder of the life available to him. Transference stops short of being a comprehensive explanation of the therapeutic relationship.

# CHAPTER 6

# Therapeutic Interruption

---

Therapists rarely know why a patient in long-term psychotherapy suddenly fails to keep his appointment and terminates treatment; or why another patient fails to improve with a highly qualified psychotherapist, but does improve, sometimes remarkably, with one recognizably inferior in training. In the same vein, we do not know the specific circumstances which impel us to refer a patient in the midst of a long-term psychotherapy to another psychotherapist. These and similar questions were posed by the referral of mid-stream patients to me, by my referral of such patients to others, and by the self-referral of patients who had abruptly left psychotherapists whom I greatly respected. I call these generic situations Therapeutic Departures, and I want now to attempt to define the parameters involved in such departures.[1]

---

[1] I am not concerned here with the manifest situation where the psychotherapist may be threatened by the patient's homosexual or heterosexual, paranoid or similar impulses, and thus refers the patient to others or the pa-

The selection and retention of the long-term patient follows the laws of congruence, that is, the similarities and dissimilarities of the unconscious structure of the two participants. It would of course be absurd to say that no patients can be given psychotherapy without congruence. But in the treatment of a chronic schizophrenic patient, for example, it cannot be expected that both participants could meet and handle the often bone-breaking vicissitudes and hardships without some unconscious "pull" to be together. Particularly where a choice of life or death confronts the patient (the question of suicide which regularly arises as part of such treatment), the psychotherapist must become a participant and not an observer. He must enter important aspects of the life of the patient and allow the patient to enter aspects of his own.

I have noted that psychotherapists who treat schizophrenic patients can be distinguished in several ways from other psychotherapists. Such distinctions have not been scientifically defined, but they seem to be related to the following qualities: A deep courage to face the implications of Eros and Thanatos; a poetic artistry in treatment backed by an acceptance of the humorous aspects of life; a deep and essential humanity which embraces the entire life principle; and a schizoid or sometimes schizophrenic quality stored but available for use if needed.

The psychotherapist who goes beyond the "mask of intimacy" is one who seeks to affirm his own creativity with every long-term patient and is compelled to do this in the same way that a writer is compelled to write. As long as he does, Therapeutic Departure does not usually occur. It is only when his own growth stops that the question of fees, appointments, hostile feelings, and similar countertransferences appear. (One of the most prevalent

---

tient leaves of his own accord. I am more interested in the indigenous and unconscious need to relegate patients to others, or to keep them close when they should depart. Of course, these impulse phenomena carry some of this latent import, but are—at any rate, in analyzed psychotherapists—at least partially conscious, so that therapeutic departure is not totally unanticipated in such cases.

myths in psychotherapy is that the psychotherapist seeks nothing from the patient but his fee.) Thus, the feeling of communication between patient and psychotherapist is not only that of sending and receiving on the same wave length, but that the communicated message promotes the existence of both.

Selecting a patient and retaining him in long-term psychotherapy is founded upon certain assumptions which should be examined:

(1) Because psychotherapy is a transferential situation involving the therapist as mother-surrogate, and because the patient's mother is for him the "Only One," it devolves upon the psychotherapist to assume the role of the Only One. And, furthermore, since the patient's mother was given to him under somewhat mysterious, sphinx-like circumstances which he never really fully comprehended, he believes that the psychotherapist came to him in the same way and that the relationship is similarily an endogenous lifetime one.[2] Although most of us know better, we soon come to accept the role of the Only One and each of us firmly believes that only his sensitivity, insight, and feeling can cure the specific patient. The hazards of our particular profession are such that traps of this nature are abundant.

(2) The second assumption, a corollary to the first, is that one psychotherapist at a time, and one only, can bring about the rebirth process and the growing-up of the patient. The psychotherapist believes that only one person at one moment can therapeutically raise the child in terms of developmental sequence and continuity. Any possible collaboration with another psychotherapist can only be cross-sectional, consultative, and time-limited. Relinquishment of the patient comes only with death or total disablement of the therapist, and the patient's Therapeutic Departure, should it occur, is experienced as a failure even though it might have important constructive aspects.

[2] This expectation is exemplified by a patient who, when she felt that I was defecting in positive regard, would say, "But you are my therapist!" as though she were saying, "But you are my mother!"

(3) Psychotherapy is a temporal coordinate of communal hours which congeals into an epoch in the lives of both participants. Patients speak of "giving a part of their lives" to psychotherapy, and psychotherapists who work with schizophrenics sometimes feel they have given something "personally intrinsic" to the patient. The assumption challenged here is that long-term psychotherapy can be delivered as a temporal package of so many sittings or hours, and that when the package is tied, the patient is completely treated. The true situation is that psychotherapy is not an epoch but a stream which ebbs and surges in an almost timeless way like life itself. Without this point of view, psychotherapy can often lead to feelings of therapeutic failure if therapeutic goals are not reached on the internalized schedule which both the patient and psychotherapist have.

(4) Our final assumption is that psychotherapy takes place in the consulting room and nowhere else. Living-out and acting-out are seen as inimical to the cure, and the psychotherapist usually asks that all energies be brought to the sessions. The focus is on the regressive transference neurosis, and interpersonal actions with significant figures in the patient's life outside the consulting room are considered relatively unimportant. In this sense an intensive love affair in the life of the patient would be more apt to be involved in the treatment if it had negative rather than positive aspects.

The assumptions upon which these beliefs rest are slowly being undermined by newer developments in psychotherapy of the polyadic type and by our increasing existential psychological understanding of the psychotherapeutic process. Indeed, in certain forms of group therapy it has become manifest that the healthy portion of the sick person's ego ministers to the sick aspects of other patients' egos, a phenomenon believed impossible a few years ago. Today we would be more inclined to wonder whether psychotherapists were not interchangeable; whether a temporary "Other" really need be the Only One; whether psychotherapy is time-packaged; and, finally, whether the analytic abstractions of "life in the consulting room" and "life in the world" are not purely artificial ones.

63

If we seek more than the remission of symptoms, as more and more patients are demanding of us, then individuation or the highest form of personal creativity can never be obtained without the connivance of the non-analytic environment in a way we have barely begun to recognize.

Recent formulations of the psychotherapeutic dynamic place the emphasis upon the person of the psychotherapist. Certain unique personality variables permit the psychotherapist to bring specific techniques to bear upon the patient, and these are backed by a more or less adequate theory. However, studies apparently reveal similar therapeutic outcomes with varying theories and methodologies. There is the X-factor in the psychotherapist's personality itself which, using Rogers as an example, can be called "unconditional positive regard." A fairly substantial list of X-factors similar to positive regard could be arrived at and all definitely related in some fashion to therapeutic outcome.

The difficulty with a personality X-factor is the assumption of constancy and universality. Suppose, for instance, that the X-factor applied to only certain phases of the psychotherapeutic process, and was indeed detrimental to others; or suppose that instead of X there were $X_1$, $X_2$, $X_3$, . . . $X_{inf}$ in a highly complex and variable arrangement. Each patient's therapeutic grid would then consist of X and highly unique X-fractions applied with some artistry and appropriateness. Even the best of therapists, however, lack certain of the necessary X-fractions. The psychotic (and neurotic) unconsciously come to recognize the deficiencies but they nevertheless need them for their own completeness. And the fact that these personality fractions may be missing does not go completely unrecognized by psychotherapists themselves for they reactively provide alter-ego complements. Each of us maintains in cognition one or two "good" therapists to whom we refer our patients when things go badly. We support such referral egos by verbalizing that Dr. Leftwich is particularly good with oral characters, Dr. Dimitri with the anally fixated, and Dr. Cohen with the Oedipally disturbed. (These names are fictitious and exemplary only.) The actual state of affairs, of course, is that Drs. Leftwich, Dimitri, and Cohen are auxiliary therapeutic egos when we cannot bring the treatment to a conclusion. They provide the needed X-fractions when, for one reason or another, we do not completely suffice. Obviously such a state of affairs is rarely admissible to ourselves, let alone to our colleagues.

One of the most secretive aspects of psychotherapy is that of referral. There are almost no studies with which I am familiar that reveal just how patients find their way to specific psychotherapists, or how they go from one therapist to another. I have observed that re-referral is most often made consciously for unconscious reasons, and that a secondary gain is involved. The unconscious of the psychotherapist contrives in one way or another to rid itself of the annoying patient, that is, the one who needs $X_1$, $X_2$, $X_3$, . . . $X_{inf}$, by referral to an auxiliary therapeutic ego, or by making it difficult for the patient to return in the old way. We may get bored, indifferent, or angry, not only when the patient is resistive or doesn't grow on schedule, but also when both participants sense that an X-fraction necessary to the patient's recovery is missing.

The patient who sees a highly qualified and motivated psychotherapist often does not improve either to his satisfaction or that of the psychotherapist. There can be no question of the latter's competence and willingness, or of the patient's openness to verbal therapy; however, the patient does not progress, and the psychotherapist's own growth remains on a plateau from which neither can move. Neither of the participants knows how to break the impasse. Finally, with considerable reluctance, the patient goes to someone else who may be as qualified or even less so than the primary psychotherapist. To the patient's surprise, and to the psychotherapist's chagrin, the treatment now moves successfully to a conclusion. Such progress needs to be explained.

I have already alluded to the X (personality) factor in psychotherapists and suggested that its components were $X_1$, $X_2$, $X_3$, . . . $X_{inf}$. I also pointed out that it is not yet possible to define these with any scientific precision, but some attempt must be made in the form of appropriate hypotheses. One such X-fraction which has suggested itself to me is what I call "Therapeutic Analyzers" and "Therapeutic Synthesizers."

Psychotherapists are both Therapeutic Analyzers and Therapeutic Synthesizers. All of them reduce and reconstruct. However, one is primarily either an Analyzer or a Synthesizer. These ego-orientations are world-designs around which attitudes, feelings, and values become organized. While they are probably orientations learned at a very early age, they become strongly fixed and soon fall out of awareness.

Dr. Hymovitz is a Therapeutic Analyzer. He stresses Aristotelian logic in the reduction of behavioral events to their lowest common denominators. In doing so he is a Western scientist, a logical positivist who, like the physicist, seeks the answers to the problems of life in ever-smaller structures. In a sense his is a deep and committed search for the monads of existence, and he finds security in the unitary nature of things rather than in totalities.

Therapeutic Analyzers see phenomena as causal chains and attempt to form relationships between many diverse events in terms of process causality. As positivists they seek generalizations which can become behavioral laws. Nothing is given, except raw nature, and they are wary of the subjective aspects of life. For centuries they suffered from the constraints of "given" theological truths. Now they are compelled to find their own. Their guide is demonstration and repeatability and they will not yield from this. Will, purpose, and values are looked upon with suspicion as metaphenomena not scientifically provable. The phenomenological and gestalt points of view interest them as aspects of the philosophy of science, but they consider such approaches arcane and metaphysical. In Binswanger's terms, a tree would not ordinarily be perceived by a scientific Analyzer as a nesting place for robins, a place under which to be romantic, or a source of food, but rather as a biological example of cellular structure, photosynthesis, or plant classification.

The Therapeutic Analyzer in his work plays a superb game similar to Hesse's Bead Game[3] in which the monads of the life history are the pawns, rooks, knights, bishops, and, of course, the king

[3] Hesse, H. *Magister Ludi* (trans. M. Savill). New York: Ungar Publishing, 1949.

66

and queen. He is fascinated by the inherent and potential arrangements of the monads and the strategies and tactics involved in the Game. The outcome of therapy, as in Hesse's book, is a form of "win or lose," but for considerably high stakes in view of the economic cost, time, and wear and tear. Often the outcome is a feeling of release through victory, as it is for the Bead Player, and a still higher Bead problem to solve. It is the Game and not the Player which counts. This may also account for the curious fact that champion chess players seem to be fairly nondescript personalities as social or ego ideals.

Therapeutic Synthesizers prefer the whole to the part and consider the former phenomenologically different from the sum of the latter. They search for the "standing forth" in behavior, the numinous, and react to it with inner subjectivity rather than objectivity. Feeling and life tone rather than rationality may be their guide, and they introspect rather than prospect for supporting evidence. With one eye focused on the demands of culture and the other on personal freedom, they often have difficulty with binocular fusion. Their approach to the reconstruction of a life is often like the poets': One must not analyze the content or the structure too closely, and only the total overriding or transcending texture of the poem is important. For them mental disease is rather a failure in the fulfillment of a life than an invasion of pathogens. They are interested in fusion rather than fission, prefer complex molecular structures to simple ones, and make few distinctions between subject and predicate and subject and object.

If the course of psychotherapy is represented by a straight line with beginning and terminal points, then this line can be arbitrarily divided into units or parts. We know from empirical studies and clinical experience that cross-sectional samples of psychotherapy taken at various points along the line vary in process, content, closure. The "end" of psychotherapy is different from the "beginning," as is the "middle" from both. Although the psychotherapist is aware of this and adjusts his methodology to fit the hypothetical point on the line, the assumption is that his unique contribution, the X, is a constant throughout. While "unconditional positive regard," one might say, may fluctuate several degrees during the course of the psychotherapy, its "basic trust" aspects never vary. My contention is that such assumptions of constancy are not necessarily correct. In the case of analysis and synthesis as the X-fraction, a patient may need 60% analysis and 40% synthesis, and not 100% of either. The proportions of analysis to synthesis vary with the patient, his problem, and his needs, but both aspects of treatment are indigenous to the "cure." There can be no "cure" where a new way of being-in-the-world is not discovered. This involves synthesizing into a more effective whole the ideas, images, affects discovered analytically earlier.

If our hypothetical linear representation reveals that the patient has had 60% of his treatment from a Therapeutic Analyzer but now requires the remaining quantum to be synthesis, an impasse may be reached if his psychotherapist is primarily an Analyzer. Under such circumstances the patient may not return when he finds a Therapeutic Synthesizer. In place of this, the psychotherapist's unconscious may contrive a referral of the patient to the therapeutic alter-ego, or will make a total rejection in the form of termination possible. But the point so often overlooked is that the work of the Therapeutic Analyzer is not lost, and is not a failure but a necessary prelude to the synthesis to follow.

There is much that is weak in my formulation of the "wandering analysand" problem: It oversimplifies a most complex problem; it suffers from the generic weaknesses of the typologies of Jung,[4] Kretschmer,[5] Sheldon,[6] and Spranger;[7] analysis and syn-

[4] Jung, C. G. *Psychological Types*. New York: Harcourt, Brace, 1933.
[5] Kretschmer, E. *Physique and Character* (trans. W. J. H. Sprott). New York: Harcourt, Brace, 1925.
[6] Sheldon, W. H., Stevens, S. S., and Tucker, W. B. *The Varieties of Human Physique: An Introduction to Constitutional Psychology*. New York: Harper, 1940.
[7] Spranger, E. *Types of Men* (trans. P. J. W. Pigors). Halle: Niemyer, 1928.

thesis are probably not pure components, and analysis may have its inherent synthetic aspects and synthesis its analytic components. Finally, psychotherapists may be able to assume analytic or synthetic stances much more readily than I have supposed. Yet examination of the lives and therapeutic styles of considerable numbers of psychotherapists reveals that Analyzers and Synthesizers do exist. They manifest themselves professionally in such widely discrepant postures as the classical psychoanalytical members of the American Psychoanalytic Association, and the existentially oriented psychoanalysis influenced by Heidegger and others. The former, I would say, are predominantly Therapeutic Analyzers, the latter Therapeutic Synthesizers. Both have been trained in classical psychoanalytical method and both represent extreme ends of universal therapeutic postures. The Therapeutic Synthesizer is, to my way of thinking, more apt to become a Neo-Freudian because of his discomfort in working at odds with his own world-design which is not highly reductionist.

If our formulations are at least heuristic, then the assumptions given at the beginning of this chapter must be revised: Long-term psychotherapy may involve multiple therapists, if not serially then conjointly; the Only-One concept becomes henceforth impossible; psychotherapy must be seen as a process occurring over a lifetime (just as biological healing never stops until death itself supervenes), and, above all, it cannot take place arbitrarily on scheduled or blocked-out time; and, lastly, the total life space will be used therapeutically both in and outside of the consulting room. The implication is that the psychotherapy of the future may not merely apply to disease but may be used for the promotion of all existence in which one will be both analyzed and synthesized to be whole.

A psychotherapist thus incurs the obligation to "know himself" even beyond what is currently required. He must not only be aware of the usual countertransference hazards but also of the missing X-fractions which, at least today, seem to be the important distinctions between widely diverse theories and methodologies. The patient must not be taken as a gross entity, and psychotherapy itself needs better definition. Above all, our reluctance to use new treatment designs involving other therapists, when either the patient or psychotherapist requires it, must be altered.

# CHAPTER 7

# Acting-Out Behavior

Acting-out behavior in psychotherapy is invariably considered an intrusion into the treatment. It complicates the therapeutic process, brings extraneous people or society into it, and diverts necessary psychic energy to the outside environment. Psychotherapists attempt to control or limit it by forbidding or mitigating major social or economic decisions, such as marriage, divorce, or a new business merger, during certain phases of the treatment process, and all psychotherapists are on the watch for it. Indeed, it has often appeared to me that acting-out constituted a considerable part of the phobic countertransference structure which some of us fall heir to in this critical work.

The patient quickly comes to know that the psychotherapist is only mildly interested in his life outside of the therapy, and that the therapist may even see such life as an obstacle to treatment. The psychotherapist hypothesizes the neurosis as a conflict between intrapsychic elements which must be worked through between the participants in his office and not anywhere else. If this is overstating the situation, I can only allow as an exception "a grudging recognition that the patient does something after he leaves the hour but what he does is not clear and furthermore there is not the time to find out." If the patient lives rather than thinks out his conflicts, through what I call molar behavior, then the psychotherapist must convert behavorial acts into their psychic equivalents so that they become manageable and manipulatable on the treatment scene.

Unfortunately, this state of affairs has created problems of its own. For example, Stierlin[1] brings up the problem of how analytic insight is converted to life insight and postulates a "creative dialectic" between conscious thinking and unconscious affective life. Fingarette[2] mentions that the Freudian "wish" is tantamount to the act, for the guilt from a "wish" and an "act" is held to be identical. Freud himself was astounded, and even traumatized, when he found that the incest his hysterical patients uniformly reported could not be verified in deed. He accounted for this by assuming the equivalence of fantasy and deed.

More serious still is that this dualism of wishes, unconscious drives and fantasies, and actual molar behavior, has radiated from psychoanalytic theory to anthropology (used here in the European sense of "the science of man") so that the dichotomies of "inner" and "outer," "subject" and "object," "vertical" and "horizontal," have become reified as major constructs of behavior. The question then arose as to their transitivity, that is, how progress is made across one condition to the other. In a sense, the total phenomenological person was grossly partialed out for better comprehension or handling. The skin, insignificant epidermal tissue, became the boundary of critical human importance; the anal, oral, urethral, genital, and other orifices became primary because this was where

---

[1] Stierlin, H. "Analytic Insightfulness and New Life Experience." In Burton, A. (Ed.), *Modern Psychotherapeutic Practice*. Palo Alto: Science and Behavior Books, 1965.

[2] Fingarette, H. *The Self in Transformation*. New York: Basic Books, 1963, p. 153.

"inner" and "outer" met. In fact, the Freudian index of psychological maturity devolved on which orifice was prepotent in the hegemony of the ego. Freud in this way indirectly added to Western man's burden by splitting him without recognizing that the most fundamental wish of all is the ancient and cosmic one of the unity of self and world.

Psychoanalytic psychotherapy has always had difficulty with the "leap" from the couch to the living world. Many case histories have as their conclusion: "The patient could not apply his analytic insights to his environment." By this is meant that the treatment went well except that the patient could not make the extrapolation from the therapist to his parents, spouse, children, employer, peer groups, or others. For me, this constitutes a failure of synthesis, of the integration of the ego aspects of treatment, and not failure of the analysis as such. Something, or some force, congeals and unifies the ego so that it can again become the executive of the personality in the living world; very little, however, is said about this phase of psychotherapy in classical texts. It is as though we believe that in some metapsychological way insight carries the instrumentation for its own application.

Acting-out is a suborder of molar behavior and it usually has an aura of the antisocial, the antipersonal, or the antitherapeutic. But our private patients are very rarely antisocial, hardly antipersonal, and certainly not antitherapeutic. Nevertheless, we fear possible misbehavior. Acting-out does have specific aggressive social possibilities in the form of incest, cannibalism, murder, rape, homosexuality, and suicide, and furthermore, often such behavior is punishable by law. No psychotherapist wants to involve himself or his patients with the law, for the law interprets literally rather than symbolically.

The problem, however, is much more subtle than this. In another chapter in this book I show that American psychoanalysts are more defensive about death (their patients' possible death as well as their own) than comparable peer theologians. They defend against the reality of this existential fact in various unconscious ways

73

and cannot easily consider it for themselves or their patients. Yet psychotherapy forces the patient to evaluate his life and often brings him to the point of despair which is the contemplation of suicide. Thanatophobia is much more difficult to handle practically than Erotophobia, and so acting-out has to be proscribed for control purposes. But this procedure may be incorrect. The treatment process admittedly mobilizes the most primitive impulses in the patient and the patient (and the community) must be protected. This is a cardinal principle. Unfortunately, the protection often goes too far, and it is possible that it is the psychotherapist rather than the patient who really seeks the protection. This, in my understanding, is a serious countertransference which must be understood before we can become adequate therapists.

Similarly, in Chapter Eight I analyze historically the taboo of touching the patient which extends even to the elemental social grace of shaking hands with him. Freud uniformly shook hands with his patients and even stroked their foreheads. There are medical practitioners called surgeons who do nothing but "touch the body," and others, called psychoanalysts, who never do at all (if they can help it). But both have cultural approval, if not a licensed mandate, to "touch the body." This countertransference phobia of keeping one's distance from the patient is beginning to break down in the psychotherapy of schizophrenia, but it is still prevalent. Its unconscious rationale is that the patient cannot be cured by a "laying-on-of-the-hands" but only by a "laying-on-of-the-mind."

While murder, rape, cannibalism, and incest are deterrents to permitting patients full expression, they do not in themselves justify the severest limitations which contemporary psychoanalytic psychotherapy places on acting-out. It was Fenichel, I believe, who said that "a neurotic is one who doesn't take action." If this is so, then action should be encouraged within the framework of psychoanalytic theory.

Psychotherapy is a non-violent, passive-feminine occupation. By this I mean that it takes place in a setting of therapeutic passivity with internalized images, ideas, and affects as the interpersonal currency. Historically, those social-philosophical movements which have had the greatest and most prolonged influence on man have been the passive-benevolent, incorporating ones rather than campaigns won on the battlefield. Contrary to opinion Freud was a gentle passive man who valued ideas over action, and whose own attitudes illustrate an accepting approach not only to life but also to the cultural climate of the intellectual Jew in Vienna. Freud rarely acted out, and very few psychotherapists do so generally in the sense of expressing impulses outside of a cognitive structure. At a meeting of five hundred psychoanalysts some time ago, I did not notice one whose hands showed the effects of heavy manual labor, and none had apparently worked in a steel mill, as a lumberjack, or as a professional football player. Psychotherapy, in common with its Judeo-Christian origins, emphasizes an inner organization and tranquility in which the environment is reduced to a subordinate or supportive role. Psychotherapy may thus be contrasted with pragmatism and behaviorism which imply drives converted to direct action or molar behavior.

Within passivity there is always femininity. Most psychotherapeutic patients are women, although most of the practitioners are men; the medium of exchange is talk (considered a feminine prerogative); emotion and affect are the problem (from the Greek *hysteria,* womb); and the classical position is supine (the one in which woman best comes to fruition). Again, in the history of mankind the role of femininity has been receptivity, docility, sensitivity, and utility, within quite narrow confines. Femininity, at least until recently, never initiated, carried out, or acted out in the world without the penalty of disfiguration or death.

The passive structure of psychoanalysis predisposed it to an aggressive theory and a passively correlated remedial technique. Not only did the technique come to consist of such abstractions as wishes, fantasies, and archaic images, but the patient was not even permitted to look at his benefactor. There is much in Freudian theory that is aggressive (id), but it is an aggression from a passive fortification, so that a panpsychism replaces what should rightly be a molar experiencing. The wish, and its analogues, become the central point of theory, and the molar experience behind the wish, of secondary moment. Rebellion as a prescription is confined to the image of rebellion; however, it should be noted that the great rebellions of history have been those in which men have actually died for their conflicts. To break an ingrained habit, it usually does not suffice to break only the psychic representation of that habit. The habit must be broken in its habitual-behavior aspect, which means the acting-out of the behavior. Such examples highlight our thesis that a wish has a molar coordinate which is not far behind it, and both together constitute the meaningful unity of behavior. To cope with one is actually to deal with the other.

If the concept of the transference is that the psychotherapist eventually comes to stand for a historic mother or father to the patient, then the therapist cannot be the belittling, frightened, double-binding, original parent. He must be something more if he is to be therapeutically effective.

There is some increasing evidence[3] that the pathogenic agent in the neurotic and psychotic disorders is neither a specific traumatic event, nor a rejecting mother as such, nor even an early environment with muddled or double-bind communication, but a total maternal milieu which counters all spontaneity and creativity. While the pathogens may consist of any or all of the above, they become virulent only under specific facilitating circumstances. These circumstances are a subtle and extremely complex milieu which denies growth, creativity, and freedom to the child. Such denial can come either in the service of love or in the service of hate and it makes little difference which. In either case, the unique and creative configuration of the developing child is shifted toward pathology by any extraordinary stimulus.

A creative and spontaneous child is a most frightening thing to a mother who is herself not spontaneous. In child analysis it is not unusual for the parents to terminate treatment just when the

[3] Pearce, J., and Newton, S. *The Conditions of Human Growth.* New York: Citadel Press, 1963.

child is discovering his own creative spontaneity. The preoccupation of mothers with schedules, rituals, groups, has the basic function of a defeating conformity in which almost every impulse needs to be accounted for in some ledger or other, and all true creative spontaneity strictly channeled or inhibited. Suppose, for example, the child's proper growth called for him to stroke his anus regularly; that, indeed, he needed to know that he had one; and that it had an important function in his existence. Very few mothers would permit such behavior. But stroking one's anus can be non-sexual, at least in the primary genital sense, and it need not be olfactory. It is analogical to the stimulation of the mucous membrane of the lip, which is accepted, widely practiced, and even encouraged in present-day society. While this example may be somewhat gross, the principle may be valid.

If you observe children at play, and observe mothers observing their children at play, you come to see that the play of the child creates anxiety in the mother. She attempts to limit not only the child's playmates, but the kind of play experience he has. However, play serves a vital personal and socializing function; it constitutes ideation and molar behavior with all cultural strictures abridged. It is an enclave of existence in which the self is totally immersed in its own being without regard to the arbitrary cultural curtailment of freedom, and this is what the mother fears.

The problem becomes compounded because psychotherapists are not noted for their own creative spontaneity or play capacity. In fact, the process of becoming a psychotherapist has seemed to me, in its more doctrinaire aspects, to be one in which creative spontaneity is purposefully sacrificed to rationality. The psychotherapist is himself a product of a mother and a culture which stress control, rationality, orderliness, predictability, and conformance at the expense of the creative expression of the deepest feelings and urges. It is thus understandable that psychotherapists seek a comparable posture for their patients which loving but creatively unspontaneous mothers thought best for their children. The American novelist F. Scott Fitzgerald once wrote that while he well recognized his chronic alcoholism and neuroticism (which finally reduced him and his artistry to nothingness), he never sought help from a psychotherapist because he felt his gifts would be analyzed away in the process. This attitude is not uncommon among gifted artists and highlights my thesis.

The intrinsic need for cognitive closure by psychotherapists makes a "tight little circle" appear mandatory. But psychotherapy by its very nature may be open-ended. No psychotherapy is really ever finished so long as life processes continue. The stopping point is arbitrary and indeterminate; what determines it is the patient's capacity to take up the joy and burden of being man with a new meaning. He will continue to rebel, but in a less neurotic way. Neurotic problems are, after all, only small problems within the context of still larger ones.[4] The problems which pleasure, pain, and power bring to men are only the individually conscious components of a broader evolutionary schema. Creative spontaneity is possible for the individual when he has come to terms not only with neurotic but with existential despair as well. This means that the patient has the opportunity of encountering all of the parataxes, inconsistencies, and paradoxes of life as presently constituted.

Life cannot be lived in the consulting room and the "transference mother" must not inhibit the creative work of life outside it. The psychotherapy is the subtle and unique wedding of both the symbolic transference and the molar act, and it is this synthesis which makes the cure possible. We sometimes tend to forget the latter radical of the equation. The psychotherapist should see molar behavior and acting-out as an adjunct rather than a hindrance to the treatment process. He cannot afford to be the "transference mother" who, in the fashion of the historical reality, deprives the child of the creative tension of play in therapy while offering him protection, support, and self-cognition. This would be a denial of the potential of the unconscious.

In the final analysis evolution can serve as a guide to inter-

---

[4] Few neurotics presented themselves for treatment in London during the peak bombings by the Nazis in the last war.

current social behavior. Teilhard de Chardin[5] has convincingly shown that in the history of living matter the grand evolutionary design is a grandiosity of forms, an overplethora of movement in the species until those with maximum adaptation evolve for survival and further evolvement. Psychotherapy is stifling itself at a critical period of evolvement because it has denied itself the full phenomenon of man in his creatively molar aspects.

[5] Teilhard de Chardin, P. *The Phenomenon of Man.* New York: Harper, 1961.

# CHAPTER 8

# Artistic Productions in Psychotherapy

The familiar model of psychotherapy is the verbal therapeutic dialogue. The strictly verbal model, however, may not be the most efficient way to relieve the patient of distress, and there may be incidental factors which force patients into the stereotyped process. American psychotherapists have been much less receptive than Europeans to the use of painting, plastic materials, and written productions in psychotherapy.

"Written productions"[1] are not themselves the treatment of the patient. All treatment forms have their accoutrements which must not be confused with the actual treatment. Written production are nothing more or less than adjunctive processes which help to implement a theory of human change. If we believe, for example, that the repression of an instinct is at the source of a symptom-complex, then any procedure which relieves that repression must be

[1] I use the term "written productions" in the text to encapsulate all artistic productions that are useful in psychotherapy.

countenanced as one aspect of the treatment based upon repression theory.

Whatever the specific goals of psychotherapy may be, they involve increased freedom for the patient to function, and a greater creativity for him. But it has only been in the last decade that serious attempts have been made to relate creativity to the psychotherapeutic process. Even now, therapists acknowledge only with considerable hesitation that they might have something to learn from the artist and his creative processes. Some of the best clinical descriptions of psychopathology come not from clinicians but from such gifted writers as Kafka, Poe, Nietzsche, Kierkegaard, Baudelaire, Dostoevski, among others. However, artists' insights are neglected, although it is covertly acknowledged that psychotherapy may be as much an art as a science.

I have observed in my treatment work that most patients, and particularly schizophrenic patients, want to be writers or painters. They reveal this often indirectly in the later stages of therapy when their long dormant creative resources are being challenged by new existential vistas. They do not necessarily want the writer's success, but they seek rather to express their innermost being in the way great artists do. They want recognition not for commercial possibilities but for their uniqueness as people. For example, they select the writer as a model because they have in the past, in suffering or joy, identified with one or another hero of a novel and felt that that particular author looked deeply into their feelings. Identification must also explain in part why so many books are written by people who have completed their psychoanalysis or were recently released from hospitalization.

Recent studies, such as that of Hollingshead and Redlich,[2] reveal what was already suspected: The person who comes for psychotherapy is a culturally selected person, and it is with such a person that therapists do their best work. Presumably the other broad segments of society who need treatment take their conflicts

[2] Hollingshead, A. B., and Redlich, F. C. *Social Class and Mental Illness.* New York: Wiley, 1958.

elsewhere. From a therapeutic point of view there are thus two broad types of membership in society: the psychotherapeutic-minded and the non-psychotherapeutic-minded. One of the things distinguishing the two groups is probably that the psychotherapeutic-minded have the capacity for a certain sensitivity and artistry in life and need to verbalize it. This capacity to feel and to verbalize what one feels is the province of the writer, and in this way the writer and psychotherapist are similar.

The writer in today's world has his share of mental conflicts, possibly more than his per-capita allotment, and he often uses his artistic medium to complete himself rather than coming to psychotherapy.[3] A case in point is Henry Miller. Miller represents a special form of expatriate whose existence was stifled by the things he believed dehumanizing in our culture. These conditions were, among others, the dehumanization of man by the machine, the drive for money and power, the failure of Protestantism as a religious force, the absence of meaning in sexuality, and the low esteem in which the creative person was held in the United States. What makes Henry Miller a good example for my thesis is that despite the immense void his work encountered, and the overwhelming social disapproval at the time, he persisted and made a distinctive contribution to literature. At thirty-nine he gave up a career as a personnel administrator to devote himself to full-time writing in Europe without resources or promise of any kind, and in this way he brought himself to fruition. I would like to think that had he gone to a psychotherapist instead of emigrating, we

[3] This is not to say that all writers are neurotic or that they must be so to be successful writers. Nor do they all write as a form of treatment. But George Orwell insists that the writer writes because he has to as a form of self-integration and can do nothing else. See *A Collection of Essays by George Orwell*. Garden City: Doubleday, 1954, pp. 313–320.

There is a point of view, however, that claims that when the writer is neurotic his production, by definition, ceases to be good writing. It is difficult to concur in this point of view, for some of the world's fine writing has been done by writers in the throes of anxiety and conflict. In America one immediately thinks of F. Scott Fitzgerald, James Agee, Thomas Wolfe, and Ernest Hemingway—as well.

would still have all of his literary productions, but I believe that some of his literary efforts might have been lost in "working through."

Sigmund Freud was also a writer, and he also was never psychoanalyzed. His systematic "written productions" not only gave psychoanalysis to the world but integrated him sufficiently so that his considerable anxieties never forced him to deviate from his goals. He found a satisfactory treatment by writing it down. The cases of Miller and Freud are not rare instances, for the success of many writers has also been a psychic growth.

Patients have varying barriers to participation in psychotherapy and such barriers must be surmounted in various ways. This is illustrated by a patient who would come regularly to treatment but would remain on the threshold of the office unable to enter. Nothing could induce her to enter the room. Finally, she brought a friend who pushed her across the threshold. Thus immersed, she calmly sat down and began free associating. It is important to get the patient in treatment any way one can. If "written productions" further the goals of treatment, they should be considered as an adjunctive technique.

American psychotherapists are a part of American culture and they demonstrate both its strengths and weaknesses. There is in this culture a generalized hostility and suspicion of the writer, and his productions are usually demeaned in comparison with other "products." This hostility may be a part of the devaluation of all things intellectual, and operates to some extent in the rejection of the patient's "written productions" as an aid to treatment. The "written production" also challenges the psychotherapist's own creativeness and temporality, and he may not have much of either to give. Furthermore, "written productions" tend to force the psychotherapist toward two considerations, neither of which he may be particularly interested in considering. In the first, he may have to retreat from the screen or passive position in which he has been trained, and in the second, he deepens the encounter by sharing in the creativity of the "production." All patient writers seek a special

83

kind of deep appreciation of their writing. All of these conditions challenge the conventional posture of the psychotherapist and may disturb his preparatory set.

It is significant that the use of "written productions" with one form of schizophrenic patient, the ambulatory type, is often simpler than with neurotic persons. The schizophrenic finds face-to-face communication with his psychotherapist extremely threatening for reasons I have already discussed. But he has the greatest urgency to communicate and relate material which might for exemplar purposes be called archetypal. If he gets into psychotherapy at all, he is most receptive to the use of the poem, novel, play, painting, and plastic materials of all kinds. Indeed, he often brings these unsolicited in a first approach to a thoroughgoing transference with his psychotherapist. To ignore such possibilities is not only to give up important associational materials of a fantasy nature, but to risk ultimate failure with the patient. In a real way, the patient's productions are the patient.

If the "written production" implies the possibility that the patient may subtly change the tone and direction of the therapy, there is then another aspect of the treatment which must be considered. Psychotherapy as we now conceive it is a historical process. We look for the genesis of the disorder in the patient's past and tend to dismiss the "present" and "future" as something which will take care of itself. But just as the dream is a projection of an unfulfilled present wish, so the "written production" deals with the patient's intercurrent status and future expectations without necessarily eliminating his history. My experience has been that where I have used "written productions" even sparingly in treatment I have become less concerned with the historical and more with the patient's contemporaneous behavior with me. This, I feel, is not necessarily detrimental, and in many cases it has its constructive aspects.

Possibly more important as a limitation of "written productions" is the problem of affect. In psychotherapy it often happens that we are less concerned with the conflict-statement than with the emotion with which it is made. The focus of therapy is not the conflict as such but the affect system which motors the conflict. Thus the conflict-statement can be experimentally changed while the affect remains relatively constant. What is missing in the "written production" is the affect of the comparable statement made directly in the psychotherapist's presence. Two programed tape recorders speaking to each other would in this sense not do at all.

These limitations do not rule out the use of "written productions." In the first place, every such document is written with a fantasied Other in mind. A fantasied image of this kind can often serve as a substitute therapist for short periods. Secondly, it is not intended that the patient's work be used in a vacuum, for the production is not an end itself. Finally, it is not correct that a "written production" has no affect connected with its creation; one has only to think of suicide notes, amatory epistles, and holographic wills, among other examples, to see this. A "written production" worked on during the course of therapy can be a highly emotional experience, depending on who produces it and how it is used.

Psychotherapists are prone to believe that short and periodic sessions of psychotherapy are what is curative, and that seeing the patient from one to four hours a week can be sufficient. However, I think that much more that contributes to treatment goes on between sessions than we now believe. Such therapeutic-work I term "interval-therapy." All psychotherapists have had the experience of the patient who comes to a session with an insight which a "third-ear" time-table has scheduled for several months later. His ego has so to speak manipulated things during the interval between treatment hours so that he has come to earlier fruition in a specific area of conflict.

Not much is known about such interval-therapy, possibly because it is not practical to follow the patient into his "world." In the past the interval has been treated as a lacuna and not as a part of treatment itself. I think, however, that the intervals between therapy hours are not lacunae nor are they so unorganized as they seem. There appears to be some correlation between effective interval-therapy and effective total psychotherapy.

Therapeutic intervals have a definite structure, and often the outcome of interval-therapy is predictable. The unconscious during the interval smooths its torn edges, and the ego is also busily at work. The therapeutic hour is rethought and reexperienced, and nuances missed in the hour itself become clarified and elaborated. Away from the psychotherapist, an integrative process functions which tests by action and reflection the various impulses, feelings, and images arising in the hour. Some patients are accustomed by inclination, habit, and facility to write things down. They may confine to writing tabooed thoughts which they cannot yet reveal to the psychotherapist. Writing also integrates new impulses and feelings on the pre-conscious and unconscious level below that of the rational and logical. It is beside the point to argue that the psychotherapist should use such "written productions" analytically during the hour. What is important is that the therapist should not discourage their production away from the hour. If he does so, it is my belief that the work of the interval is disturbed and something valuable for the total treatment is missed.

The therapeutic style of patients differs, and they cannot all be asked to conform to one select style of relating. There is a modicum of narcissism and rigidity in any approach to healing which maintains itself in an invariate way and thereby disregards the patient's deeper means of expression. However, the psychotherapist should not abjure peripheral techniques which may be helpful in therapy.

There are serious disadvantages to the general use of "written productions" and some of these can have a corrupting influence on the treatment. These I have summarized as follows:

(1) A "written production" displaces the emphasis from the interaction between patient and psychotherapist to a solitary activity away from the psychotherapist. In this way it is dissociative and transference-reducing.

(2) Intellect is to some extent subsidized at the expense of

affect, and the therapeutic currency tends to become ideas rather than feelings.

(3) The psychotherapist may be inherently less literate or creative than his patient and thus unable to use the medium of "written productions" at the level the patient expects. Conversely, not all patients have the capacity for "written productions."

(4) Writing may be a defense against direct confrontation. In this sense it may serve as yet another form of resistance.

(5) If a "written production" is helpful, there may be a tendency to assign more and more of the actual psychotherapy to the interval because of convenience, simplicity, and cost. The theoretical point of absurdity is reached when the patient comes, to all intents and purposes, to be treating himself.

(6) The tone and structure of the psychotherapy may be insidiously altered in a manner described above.

(7) "Written productions" are imaginal rather than actional. They focus on the interior of the person when externalizing may be the need at certain stages of treatment. In this sense they promote introspection rather than integrative action.

The advantages of "written productions" I see as follows:

(1) The preparation of a "written production" such as a diary, autobiography, short story, poem, letter, etc., by a patient is an expressive and creative act. It both analyzes and synthesizes emotion in a deeply personal way and, as such, works counter to repressive and regressive forces in the personality. It is catharsis in the best sense. It heals through its major symbolism because the unexpressible is permitted expression.

(2) The content of the "written production" provides materials for analysis similar to dreams, fantasies, projective tests, and other imaginative productions. The language of the "written production" is also as much a source of parapraxis as are slips of the tongue, forgetting, and dreams.

(3) "Written productions" further interval-therapy by providing for rehearsal of therapeutic hours. In this way they encourage the development of cognition and insight. Above all, if the

psychotherapist is the respondent to the "written production," his presence in interval-therapy is given a tangible imaginal form.

(4) A "written production" usually has a wider social base than an individual therapy session. In this sense, it is more outer-directed for it involves family, peer groups, and authority figures, to a greater extent than the sessions. Since society is the place where the patient ultimately makes his life, the "written production" permits a wider social integration of analytic material.

(5) My experience has been that, under certain circumstances, the time required for treatment may be condensed by the judicious use of "written productions."

(6) Under emergency circumstances of unavoidable separation of patient and psychotherapist, "written productions" can be used with the telephone and standby colleagues as a means of keeping the treatment in force.

(7) There are some treatment situations where the patient is silent for unbearable periods of time and does not tolerate the silence well. "Written productions" can help break the impasse.

I am certain that there are additional advantages and disadvantages to the use of "written productions" besides those I have given. I have depicted "written productions" from the broad vantage point of a generic technique rather than in terms of specific case-treatment situations. My greatest use of them has been with the diary form—excluding painting and clay—and I have asked a number of patients to keep them.

Diaries as personal documents have a history antedating psychoanalysis. Even today they have a formal place in the psychiatry of Japan.[4] The distinctive characteristics of diaries are that they are secret (modern diaries, for example, come with attached locks), provide continuity, and offer feedback systems. The need for the diary stems from the need to express something personal

[4] Arthur Koestler in *The Lotus and the Robot* (New York: Alfred A. Knopf, 1961) reports that Japanese psychiatrists ask their patients to write diaries they turn over to the psychiatrist for his perusal. It is not actually clear whether this is a diary or an autobiography.

and intense which the person feels cannot be expressed in any other way. Such expression is directed toward the writer's ego, but also toward the Other. Examination of a number of diaries reveals that their content is highly libidinal, as well as philosophic. Diaries help clarify the more critical and charged areas of life such as love, pain, marriage, parturition, and death, and this may explain why they seem more characteristic of adolescence than adulthood.

Without the factor of "secrets" there would probably be no diaries, for diaries involve a communion with the deepest aspects of the conscious self away from the object world. Fantasies are given full sway within a specific structure and "one can be" what "one is" in the diary. Diary material can be differentiated from dreams by their lowered symbolic quality and by their "quasi-rational" as opposed to unconscious function. There is less need for fictions and double-binds in diaries because the ego is basically concerned with itself and thus has less need of social defenses. Should the diary be surreptitiously read by a significant person, an upheaval can be expected, for it is as though the ego were suddenly to be denuded.[5]

The need for secrecy involves at the same time the need to reveal the "secret." The probability is that diaries would not be written if they were meant only to be seen by the writer. The diary is intended to convey significant messages to real or fictional characters when ordinary communication is completely out of the question. Life continuity is involved for the relationships in the diary are more or less stable and enduring. Feedback enters because the expectation of the writer is that the Other for whom the diary is written has a respondent diary hidden somewhere to which his is merely a refrain. Thus the diary serves as a kind of dialogue of "secret" experience not unlike psychotherapy itself.

I have used diaries in marital counseling. Much marital

---

[5] In Vladimir Nabokov's screen play of his novel *Lolita*, Lolita's mother kills herself when she reads in her husband's diary that he prefers her daughter to her. But what she really sees in his diary is the reality and absurdity of her romantic strivings. In the face of such reality, she cannot live.

counseling is done under adverse circumstances in that considerable pressure has been built up in the marriage by the time the counselees come for therapy. Often a divorce is imminent and counseling is used as a "last resort," or one of the partners is actually forced to come. One of the mates "arranges" for the counseling and the other is, so to speak, the victim of it. Both have vested interests in preserving their gains from the unhappy marriage, and both have a proprietary interest in any change which may occur. With each of them I use a number of therapeutic designs. I see them together, I see them individually, and I sometimes see them with their children, or whatever relative is resident in their home. The curious homeostasis of sickness and health in the family group becomes apparent in this way, and growing therapeutic insight comes to be rationed and distributed according to the family-system's peculiar dynamics. This makes the triadic session quite sensitive indeed, so that crucial insights come only with the most strenuous of therapeutic campaigns. Also, the passive become more passive in the hour, and the aggressive more aggressive, or there is a complete about-face allowed by the protective presence of the psychotherapist. There is in addition the reality of the carrying-on of the counseling hour at home during the marital counseling interval. In this form of interval-therapy, particularly in the earliest stages, the material of the counseling hour is used against each partner and acts as a reinforcement of the inherent pathology of the marriage.

In situations such as these, diaries have been most helpful. I ask each partner to keep a diary in "secret." Neither knows the other has been asked to do so, and I indicate that under no circumstances must the other partner read it. I myself refrain from seeing the diaries until a period has elapsed in which each partner finds he has a "secret" repository of his deepest feelings. Occasionally a counselee will bring his diary to his individual hour to quote some paragraph, but I discourage this.

It sometimes happens that the diary falls into the hands of the other partner. A period of considerable upset then supervenes in which I am apt to receive a number of phone calls or requests for extraordinary sessions. But surprisingly, I have found that the reading of the respective diaries is often the first moment in which each partner enters the private world of the other. Counseling thereafter runs a smoother course. From the diary it becomes clearer to the marital partners that the issues at combat are not the real issues at all, and rather than being indifferent in the marriage, each partner is very much involved, if not over-involved, in it. Should the diary not be found by the marital partner, its content is usually brought to the counseling anyway because of its immediacy and presence in the counselee's psyche.

I do not want to overdo the "written production" in this instance. The use of such a production involves a psychotherapist and the major contribution of the therapeutic situation, in which analysis and synthesis are both at work, which makes the use of the diary possible to begin with. The technique needs further exploration and study. But I must insist that the diary can often be helpful, if not critical, not only in marital counseling situations but in other psychotherapies as well.

# CHAPTER 9

# Touching the Patient as Mothering

As cultures evolve, the sensate qualities of immediate experience tend to be relinquished for intellectual forms of a conceptual nature. Possibly the primary exemplar of such development is language, which grows in an exceedingly complex way; lingual forms often create rather than follow reality. Deviations from such forms are looked upon as pathological although they may have existential meaning or genesis. There is nothing wrong with conceptualizing, but a concept in order to be truly communicative must carry a message on a lower level, that is, it must have emotional meaning. Primitive man had concepts, but they were more immediately related to his personal world of experience, and in this experience his body played a uniquely mediating part.

As culture attains higher social forms it desiccates itself by abstractions and reduces the immediacy of personal experience. The prevalent cry of alienation and "loss of meaning" today stems from that quality of culture which denies the body and ignores the integrative aspects of its impulses. A rather distasteful image of Muggeridge's is perhaps apropos here. If mankind consists of pigs eating at a trough, then culture is the one pig which raises its head to look around. But if the pig becomes enchanted with what he sees and fails to lower his head, he is apt to lose his piggish identification. The analogy is that man is first a biological animal and if, like Icarus, he flies too high toward the pure sun of abstraction, he will have to pay a considerable price in divorcement.

Western man has shown a progressive estrangement from his body. He tends to be less aware of it, less accepting of it, and depends to an increasing degree on prostheses and cosmetics. Unfortunately, such aids no longer have the aesthetic and religious significance of the past, and as modern devices they are only at the service of man's narcissism. The Hellenic image of the body has been lost, and there is today no group of statuary and sculpture comparable to what the Greeks left as their legacy. Even coeval athletic contests are devoid of the glorification of the body, for they are most often contests in which winning or the purse attached is the prize. Sexuality is momentarily orgastic and makes no contribution to the total bodily economy and aesthetic.

The issue has a particular and interesting ramification for psychotherapy. Psychotherapists have a horror of touching their patients. Although a psychotherapist has a license to practice medicine he abstains from any examination when his patient complains of pain. Medicine seems to have been dichotomized into those who "touch the body" and those who do not. Such dissociation may be an aspect of cultural development which medicine reflects, or it may carry its own specific medical insidiousness.[1] In this chapter I want to trace the origin of the taboo of "touching the body" and to show the taboo's influence on the current practice of psychotherapy, particularly with schizophrenic patients.

---

[1] Western cultures have been particularly susceptible to divorcement from the body, seeking higher and purer forms for ennoblement. This is not so true for Oriental and Asian cultures. It does seem that all Western men seek outside their bodies for what we might call grace or happiness.

It should be noted at the outset that the history of psychiatry ranges from "the act of doing something to the body" to such current and rarefied conceptions as Jung's archetypes. Before Freud, psychiatry was essentially the application of various physical modalities to the body in an attempt to influence the mind. Freud postulated the structure and dynamic of the psyche but kept the body and its systems as a frame of reference. His theory was a biological one, and in his practice he frequently stroked the patient's head or neck for stimulative effect, as did Groddeck and others. As far as is known, he also followed the Viennese custom of shaking hands with his patients. As psychoanalysis developed, however, it lost the "personal touch," so that distancing increased in both a literal and metaphorical sense.

Today psychotherapists[2] have a fear of touching their patients and refer them for this function when physical pain or discomfort supervenes. They avoid any physical contact, no matter how minor, and have a horror of its possibilities. Accompanying such psychotherapeutic dissociation, however, surgery and internal medicine have increased, so that one group touches with fervor and the other not at all. That the problem has not gone totally unrecognized is seen in the current emphasis on psychosomatic medicine, which attempts to bridge the hiatus, and in the application of psychotherapy to psychotic patients. In both of these developments, an attempt is made to return the body to the psyche.

Archaic man's existence was close to nature because he was constantly faced with the necessity of defending himself for survival. He was a part of nature, and he made few distinctions between himself and the world he lived in. This unity created few barriers between him and the natural world and the flow was constant and uninterrupted. His body was in and part of it, and he could not be

[2] The lay psychotherapist does not have the legal right to examine the body. Our argument is, however, not vitiated by this fact, for in the relatively rare instance where he does gain this right (by securing an M.D. and license to practice medicine) he does not usually avail himself of his new-founded privilege. The argument seems to me a generic one.

concerned whether he was a "subject" or an "object." When his body failed to function, he applied those remedies which came from the earth, and he used incantations or magic when his crops failed. His was the indivisible unity which made him part of a cosmic whole.

The epochs which followed brought differentiation of the self from the world, and structuralization and conceptualization of the contents of self. This had two aspects: the nature of the "internal body," and the search for a suprabody or psyche (soul). Attempts at definition went on sporadically and simultaneously in Egyptian, pre-Hellenic, Greco-Roman, Byzantine, Arabic, Oriental, and other cultures, but men were first fascinated by their inner and tangible contents. They fell busy examining organs, including the brain, and defining organic functions. Only much later did a conception of body organization and dis-organization, with corollaries of dis-ease and dis-comfort, become possible. This ultimately led to formalized conceptions of pathology and therapeutics. The latter took two forms: first, the removal of the offending part or agent, and, second, the addition to, or enhancement of, the body. Both have a respectable place in this history of medicine and still apply today in surgery and prosthesis.

While Asclepius, Hippocrates, and other pre-Socratic philosopher-physicians speculated about man's inner functions and make-up, others sought a certain agency within him, but somehow beyond his organs, which gave him a divinity in the image of his gods. Christianity captured the psyche for itself, gave it its particular bent, and ordained a metaphysical distinction between body and mind (soul), formalizing earlier Socratic, Platonic, and Aristotelian speculations. Mosaic law and the Apostles firmly saddled Western civilization with its peculiar dualistic burden which still plagues us. By so doing it applied moral legitimation to what previously had been neither base nor elevating; corporeal sin was created, and its camp followers, guilt and repression. What had been instinctual or pleasurable, that is, what the body distinctively had to offer, came to be tabooed, covertly responded to, and forced the quest for some-

95

thing higher and purer in man. But purity can only be known by its obvious dialectic opposite, dirt, which is its dynamic and which by necessity now exerts its major influence in the unconscious.

In a unique and unforeseen way Freud fostered the dualism of mind and body while attempting to preserve a monistic position. It was inevitable that the discovery that a repressed idea could lead to a bodily symptom would result in the systematic cleansing of that human storehouse, the unconscious, and the greater and greater reification of complexes as complexes. The body in psychoanalysis ultimately became a container of complexes at best, and an interference to the analysis of those complexes at worst. It got in the way of the analysis and, if it issued pain, it was to be referred elsewhere, or the pain was to be itself a subject for analysis. Thus there is today the analysis of the complex without the encumbrance of the body.

The penalty for such reification is often the reduction of the complex and the continued ill health of the patient. Since the body is not a part of the treatment, it does not subscribe to the cure. There is in this century a frantic search for the body in its totality and manifold parts, and neither the psyche nor the body alone is satisfactory for the integration of modern man. The estrangement of Western man is in a sense the estrangement from his body of which, of course, the instincts are but a part. But it goes beyond this. Man's need is not necessarily more instinctual expression, for he already has more than he has ever known, but the integration of the body and psyche on the pattern residual in every unconscious.

All of the senses act as a dynamic whole, one complementing the other in reciprocal fashion. The result is a sensory Gestalt which is the true stimulus for behavior. For one reason or another the visual, the auditory, and the gustatory have been singled out as primary sense modes, whereas the tactual and olfactory have been denied their former biological status. I have already implied that biologically no sense mode is privileged; that selection of one sense mode over another is done by man and reinforced by culture; and that the body has its own repressive dynamic. I am not concerned here with the olfactory sense. But it may be noted in passing that

96

olfaction joins tactuality in reaching the deepest layers of the psyche, and that in dreams, myth, fantasy, and hallucination, such sense modes are most prominent.

Touch is the fundament of being-in-the-world for it is the vehicle par excellence by which the person locates himself in space-time. Man is of the earth, and it is his tactual contact with the earth which gives him the base for higher-order operations. Surrendering this tactuality by flying or diving creates anxiety because "touch" is lost. Tactuality in the new-born infant is the basic orientation to the mother and, therefore, to life.[3] The child feels the mother before he sees her. He is uniquely comforted by the mother's closeness, and less so by the blurred image of her face. While nourishment comes from the breast, it is the contact and manipulation of the breast which are psychologically as important as the nourishment itself.[4] In this way the child preserves the original unity of the two bodies. Separation is more than a psychic fact: It is the actual breaking apart of what was formerly one, and all separations are symbolic of the primary one in which fusion was the rule. Tactuality ontogenetically reinforces the indivisibility and wholeness of man and counters separation.

If one enters a ward of regressed schizophrenic patients who have been hospitalized for long periods, the "noisy" silence of the ward is startling until one realizes that the arms which flail out to touch are a substituted form of communication. They want again to make tactual contact to reassure themselves of their continuity and existence. The same is true of a geriatric ward. The need to touch supersedes the need to verbalize, and offers reinforcement on a level more congruent with deficit status. The anticipation of de-

[3] Harlow has pointed out in his studies on ersatz motherhood in monkeys that the intimacy that comes from the physical contact of mother and new-born offspring is more important than the feeding itself. The infant has greater difficulty reconciling himself to the tactual loss of the mother than to any other deprivation.

[4] I have observed an adult male cat that makes periodic manipulative nursing movements to an old mop, which seems to be a regression to the tactuality he missed in an over-large litter. He is often unwilling to leave his mop for feeding.

97

cline and death in such patients forces them to cling tactually, not only to the world, but to the unconscious residuals of the mother symbiosis.

Problems of discipline with children are often displaced needs for affection. Furthermore, the child wants to be touched even at the cost of severe bodily punishment. The question on the part of parents "whether or not to spank" does not concern a form of punishment, but rather whether the body of the child should be touched. The dynamics of masochism reveal to what extent this can be carried. What should be pain and avoided becomes pleasure and is desired because of the desperate need for human contact. Thus pain becomes exquisite and is often the only tangible proof that the person exists.

Another case in point are the blind. Blind people are generally thought of as being non-erotic in character. However, it should not be difficult to become passionate about a blind person for all of the ingredients of romance could be present with the exception of the visual. In poetry and music eyes often symbolize the love relationship, and considerable funds are expended by women to enhance the enchantment of their eyes. But apart from seeing, the eye is not capable of direct sexual response as are, for example, the ear, lips, and tongue. The blind displace the visual to the tactual, and in the final analysis in sexuality it is the tactual which governs sensuality. On this basis, the blind should be more rather than less sought after erotically. Obviously, culture forces a displacement upward, to the visual, which then assumes arbitrary excitatory powers properly belonging below. Voyeurism and exhibitionism are pathological examples of displacement. In this sense, the visual constitutes a flight from the body and acts as an artificial defense against true eroticism. It is interesting to note in this regard that psychotherapy is a process in which this state of affairs is reversed: The pre-genital or displaced-genital must become genital, and hence tactual.

I would say that the problem of touching lies not so much with the patient as with the psychotherapist. It is because the psychotherapist does have a need to touch his patient that the taboo comes into play. The fear and guilt involved are more often the psychotherapist's than the patient's, and such attitudes constitute countertransference barriers to the relationship. Such countertransference is both conscious and unconscious and has personal and institutional forms. An infant can be fondled without social disapproval, but once the infant is grown the taboo asserts itself. Similarly, a very young child always has the social right to touch, but once he is grown he loses that right. Adulthood seems to bring bodily estrangement.

In the psychotherapy of schizophrenia a point is reached where the patient desires to touch the therapist.[5] I would say that if this does not occur during the course of treatment the psychotherapy is going badly. Schizophrenia is by definition regression to the primary process and to a primary narcissism. No matter how the schizophrenic condition is conceived, what the patient seeks is human relatedness, and the process of psychotherapy is the process of reestablishing such relatedness. The psychotherapist, so to speak, is the midwife of the new birth, and like all infants, the patients have expectations of being fondled. But whether such expectations can or should be met is a complex issue which needs clarification. Such psychotherapists of schizophrenic patients as Whitaker, Malone, and Warkentin,[6] Sechehaye,[7] Rosen,[8] and others apparently feel that some limited body contact is helpful during certain stages

[5] This is true not only of schizophrenic patients but of some neurotics. The situation is, however, seen in bolder relief with psychotics.

[6] Whitaker, C. A., Warkentin, J., and Malone, T. P. "The Involvement of the Professional Therapist." In Burton, A. (Ed.), *Case Studies in Counseling and Psychotherapy*. New York: Prentice-Hall, 1959. Whitaker, C. A., and Malone, T. P. *The Roots of Psychotherapy*. New York: Blakiston, 1953. Warkentin, J., and Taylor, J. E. "Case Fragment: The Experimental use of Physical Contact in Multiple Therapy with a Schizophrenic Patient." *Cong. Rep. II, International Congress for Psychiatry*, Vol. III, 1957.

[7] Sechehaye, M. A. *A New Psychotherapy in Schizophrenia: Relief of Frustration by Symbolic Realization*. New York: Grune & Stratton, 1956. Sechehaye, M. A. *Autobiography of a Schizophrenic Girl*. New York: Grune & Stratton, 1961. Sechehaye, M. A. *Symbolic Realization*. New York: International Universities Press, 1951.

[8] Rosen, J. *Direct Analysis*. New York: Grune & Stratton, 1953. Scheflen, A. E. *A Psychotherapy of Schizophrenia: Direct Analysis*. Springfield, Ill.: Thomas, 1961.

of the treatment. This sometimes involves holding hands, a caress, being nursed on the therapist's lap, a perfunctory kiss, but also pushing, kicking, tugging.

Let me assume that at a critical point in therapy I offer the schizophrenic patient my hand. Possibly this occurs when verbal communication has completely broken down, and where the therapeutic communion needs the reinforcement of a form of body language. Offering a hand to a patient has nuances on several levels which must be carefully distinguished. There is first of all the simplest acknowledgment of an encounter. (Two people meet and socially validate their meeting by a form specified by culture.) Shaking hands is a desexualized body contact which acknowledges membership in a common culture, and in a common fate. It is the earliest stage of rapport. The second level of hand-shaking involves greater awareness that two bodies are in contact for the clasp is warmer, longer, and more intense, and that a sensual element has been introduced into the relationship. The two participants see each other in more than culturally defined roles as patient and psychotherapist, and the expectation is that their encounter will lead to some additional fulfillment.

Below these two apparent levels is a third, more complex, evanescent, and almost without personal awareness. I call it the paleo-symbolic.[9] It is an immediate, felt, intuitive response between two people, undignified by speech, and involving tactual, postural, kinesthetic, and other sensory-motor cues. It carries the residuals of past human experiences and is deeply rooted in instinctual and reflexive behavior. The body, in this paleo-symbolic way, has its own economy and language, and this is why "somatic" accompanies "psycho" to form the complete conceptual unity of "psychoso-

[9] LSD seems to enhance the sense of tactuality in a florid way. One function of LSD, in the experimental treatment of schizophrenia, may be that it furthers paleo-symbolic communication. The patient is somehow freed by LSD from his tactual repressions, so that his hallucinations and delusions reveal his true bodily interpersonal needs. The therapist responds to the patient comparably as a reverberation of the patient's own temporary body freedom.

matic." The fact that such bodily communication is recognized principally under conditions of pleasure and pain does not vitiate the fact that the body speaks directly in its own right and in this consistent way.

Offering one's hand to a patient can thus have overtones which might appear to be undesirable in treatment, or it can, on the simplest level, be a reinforcement of the encounter. If the therapist is maladroit, the patient may use it to defeat treatment, or to defeat the therapist, which amounts to the same thing. These considerations combine to produce psychotherapists who may vary from "those who recoil in horror at the thought of shaking hands with a patient" to "those who are willing to 'nurse' psychotic patients if they require it."[10] Frieda Fromm-Reichmann gives the following caution to touching the patient:[11]

. . . we do not believe that it is necessary or desirable for the psychiatrist to bar responsive reactions of spontaneity from the psychotherapeutic scene, as long as his responsive facial expressions cannot be used by patients as a means of orientation inadvertently guiding their productions and behavior. Also they must, of course, be genuine responses to patients' communications and not colored by his private collateral experiences . . . At times it may be indicated and wise to shake hands with a patient or, in the case of a very disturbed person, to touch him reassuringly or not to refuse his gesture of seeking affection and closeness. However, it is always recommended that one be thrifty with the expression of any physical contact.

As a broad and probably valid generalization I would say that psychotherapists dislike their bodies at the unconscious level.[12]

[10] A colleague has related that he regularly shakes hands with schizophrenic patients who serve as subjects in his research project, but will not do so with the schizophrenic patients he has in therapy even though they may in some instances be the same subjects he has in his experiment.

[11] Fromm-Reichmann, Frieda. *Principles of Intensive Psychotherapy.* Chicago: University of Chicago Press, 1950, p. 12.

[12] State hospitals usually have nonpsychiatric physicians and psychiatrists on their staffs. Since both are physicians, the physical examination of

The body is what is born and what dies, and this is disturbing, for most of us secretly find a place for an enduring self. That is, we want to be infinite when we are finite, and anything which forces us to face our limitedness is subject to repression. The psyche can in a sense go on forever, but the body comes to an end as a part of an organic process. The difficulty, for example, of interesting physicians in a geriatric service in the mental hospital is just such a difficulty: The physician is everlastingly confronted with his mortality. Psychotherapy itself is a process which plays into the fiction of immortality, for one of the hazards of psychotherapy is chronic omniscience and everlasting perpetuity. Thus the countertransference of the body is in part the counter-identification with the patient's body and the rejection of it as mortal.

Watts[13] has ably pointed out how the "off-scene," that is, the non-assimilated individual in culture, becomes the "obscene" by a simple transformation. The emotionally ill may, in the deeper recesses, thus be equated with something dirty, either in their essence or in their behaviors. The correlation of character with bodily orifices, whose function is "disposal," is a case in point. Body orifices that dispose of waste are the "drain" aspects of humanity and are generally avoided. Since emotional problems are quite often libido problems, that is, they involve the urgencies of the body, it is the body which is considered obscene. Touching the patient may then unconsciously involve the possibilities of contamination, or of soiling the hands.

Psychotherapy promises the patient the possibilities of a reliving or reinstatement of earlier and more pleasant times, with projections into the future. Such promise, even when it is disavowed, is always inherent in the therapeutic relationship. After all current re-

---

each newly admitted patient is divided among the total medical staff. Psychiatrists, however, demur from such duties for a variety of reasons. Their discomfort in examining the bodies of new patients is, however, also unconsciously rooted in their fear and dislike of their own body, in addition to whatever other dynamic factors motivated them to become psychotherapists instead of surgeons or internists.

[13] Watts, A. W. *Nature, Man and Woman.* New York: Mentor, 1960.

search on psychotherapy is accounted for, psychotherapy still resolves itself into a relationship best subsumed by the word "love." The patient comes to the psychotherapist because he is considered an expert in the "love that heals" and because, like the good father, he can provide it and teach it without damage. And it is obvious that no significant amelioration is possible unless the borderlands and quicksands of just such an emotional (love) relationship are approached in the treatment.

If then all psychotherapy has potential erotic overtones, and no preestablished boundaries or limits to the requisite love exist, they must be set by the participants themselves. Since the transference invariably involves the Oedipal situation it becomes incestuous by a simple transformation, and countertransference counterincestuous. The transference is, moreover, a transitive relationship and involves not only the patient's projections on the psychotherapist but the psychotherapist's projections upon the patient. Since incest is taboo, touching the patient becomes impossible without the penalty of unconscious anxiety, an archaic part of all culture. Indeed, under most circumstances, the treatment has to be surrendered if this is done at all. Furthermore, there is the added phobia of homosexuality which, like incest, has its own countertransference effects.

There is sufficient social reason why the patient should not be touched. Existing codes define the conduct of patient and doctor under general and specific statutes. Judeo-Christian law recognizes the right to bodily protection of minors, the handicapped, the mentally ill, and the helpless. The bodies of such individuals can be touched therapeutically only under specific conditions which most often involve narrowly formulated diagnostic and treatment procedures. Such procedures must by law be completely divorced from erotic stimulation of any kind. Yet the psychoanalytic psychotherapist often finds the supine position on the couch the posture necessary for curing the patient. However, this is also the principal sexual position. There is a curious paradox here for it is as though the couch were needed to reinforce the strength of the taboo of touching.

The combination of unanalyzed or unanalyzable residuals in the psychotherapist, coupled with legalistic definitions of touching behavior, make it extremely difficult to be free and spontaneous in this area of treatment. The flight from the body has been a long and insidious one which psychotherapy cannot be expected to solve by itself. Yet, when we accept a schizophrenic patient for treatment, we implicitly promise to do what needs to be done for his improvement and we cannot renege on this implied contract.

My thesis is that with rare exceptions the patient need not be touched. But the psychotherapist and schizophrenic patient need to feel they can touch if they have to. Eroticism is an intention, and, if one does not intend it, it must not be construed. Freedom in therapy is the freedom to be what one is, and the freedom to act is liberating whether one acts in this way or not. This freedom is what the patient seeks, rather than the actual physical touching. Constriction reinforces frustration by adding to the blocked energy and thereby intensifying the need. Freedom from constriction leaves all media open for the therapeutic encounter and permits symbolic processes to operate. It is, moreover, surprising how little attention has been given to the function of symbols in the quieting and satisfaction of such body needs.[14]

There is, then, a symbolized or fantasied touching which meets the patient's momentary and infantile needs. Shared fantasies are communal and have effects; however, the two people in the therapeutic relationship must not be fearful of their fantasies but be free to share them. The freedom to touch is extended to the freedom to fantasy touching and in this way satisfies the need. The

[14] In psychoanalysis Marguerite Sechehaye and C. G. Jung have perhaps demonstrated this point most dramatically. Ernest Cassirer has most *generally* elaborated the function of symbols in a helpful way. Sechehaye, M. A. "The Curative Function of Symbols in a Case of Traumatic Neurosis with Psychotic Reactions." In Burton, A. (Ed.), *Psychotherapy of the Psychoses.* New York: Basic Books, 1961. Cassirer, E. *The Philosophy of Symbolic Forms* (3 vols.). New Haven: Yale University Press, 1953. Cassirer, E. *Language and Myth.* New York: Dover, 1946. Jung, C. G. *Collected Works.* New York: Pantheon (various dates).

greatest generic error in psychotherapy occurs in withdrawal from the patient rather than in going forward to him. If a handshake is required, it should be countenanced with, of course, all of the possible limitations in mind. The important thing, I must repeat, is that the psychotherapist be sufficiently free in his person to accept the responsibility of touching should it arise.

CHAPTER 10

# Fear of Death as Countertransference

Psychoanalysts are frequently uneasy about Freud's formulations concerning the death instinct. Since these conceptions came late in Freud's career, they are often attributed to the insecurities of aging or to difficult cultural experiences. Thus Eros is prominent in psychoanalytic theory, whereas Thanatos is neglected. It is not my purpose here to make a case for or against the death instinct,[1] or even to offer didactic advice on the handling of the fear of death.[2] I want rather to highlight a problem in psychotherapy not frequently seen in this perspective, and to point out its implications for treatment.

As man's powers of mass destruction have grown, so has the topical fear of death in psychotherapy. The existential philosophers

[1] This has been well done indeed by Norman O. Brown in his *Life Against Death: The Psychoanalytical Meaning of History.* New York: Random House, 1959.

[2] See Eissler, K. R. *The Psychiatrist and the Dying Patient.* New York: International Universities Press, 1955.

and psychiatrists have pointed up the growing frequency of despair and alienation in Western culture and have correlated these states with Nothingness, understood as some condition of ultimate emptiness related to death. Patients today seem to be saying with increasing frequency, "I feel as though I were dead," or, "I wish I were dead." All of us have had the experience of having a recovered psychotic patient tell us that "he was dead" during the disturbed period of his psychosis. The intrusion of death, of thanatophobia, in this way into psychotherapy makes it mandatory that its countertransference aspects be studied. The fact that every person dies means that every psychotherapist and every patient must cope with death. Thus death and its phobic aspects make an unescapable problem in psychotherapy.

For a number of reasons it seemed best to begin such a study not with the patient but with the psychotherapist. My impression had been that psychotherapists were extraordinarily, but covertly, sensitive to death, both in their personal lives and in the lives of their patients. It seemed to me that psychotherapy itself was an occupation in which living and dying paid higher symbolic premiums for both participants. Psychotherapists, however, tend to relegate matters of dying to other professions, even when such matters are a function of the patient's growth. Upon serious reflection I found that I myself held ambiguous attitudes about death and I wondered about countertransference aspects within me. An interesting case in point was my inability to complete a certain phase of this study, which involved measuring the attitudes toward death of patients currently in psychotherapy. The aid of psychotherapists could not be enlisted, for they univocally felt that allowing a questionnaire on this topic to be independently given to their patients would disturb something in their therapeutic relationship.

If psychotherapists believe in the reality principle, then they must accept the reality of Thanatos. We deny something vital to our patients and to ourselves if we obscure this part of life. Psychotherapeutic attitudes toward death seem to be handed down by training psychotherapists in a viable but unseen form, so that a closed and largely unknown system of negation is established. If training in psychotherapy provides for an analysis of the personality of the trainee, his conscious and unconscious feelings about death should also be analyzed. It is paradoxical that the psychotherapist's greatest problem with his patients—life and its vicissitudes—is often denied in his training.

The purpose of my study was to test whether Thanatos was indeed a countertransference. It seemed to me that a beginning needed to be made in this area. A number of approaches to the problem were considered and discarded as impractical. For example, it would have been relevant to study a series of dreams of psychotherapists in which death, or its symbols, appeared. Failing this I might have administered the Thematic Apperception Test, or a special projective test of Thanatos.[3] Instead, I developed a pool of brief statement-items on death which were pretested on a sample of college students and clinical psychologists. On this basis, ten of the statement items were selected as having the best potential for uncovering both manifest and latent attitudes toward death. This approach, in the final analysis, turned out to be less than perfect; however, the data are sufficiently substantial to show directionality. The statement items in the order presented are as follows:

1. Is death a beginning or an end?
2. What is the proper time to die?
3. What is the best way to die?
4. "The burial ritual is an outmoded personal and cultural device." Comment.
5. How many people would miss you were you to die today? How many would you miss were they to die today?
6. Ideally, what personal, social, and professional arrangements should be made for one's death?
7. "A feeling of immunity toward death is a *necessary* fiction for psychoanalysts (or ministers)." Comment.

[3] I have experimented in a preliminary way with such a test. It seems to offer considerable "life" material as a corollary to the Thematic Apperception Test.

8. Should an individual have the right to "choose" his own death?

9. "The inevitability of death assures man of his finiteness and weakness." Comment.

10. Do you consider discussions about death best avoided with your patients (or parishioners)?

Members of the American Psychoanalytic Association were selected as respondents because their training in psychotherapy is comparatively homogeneous and often considered to be superior. Obviously, they are not representative of all psychotherapists, and becoming a psychoanalyst is itself a selective and thus a biased process. However, psychoanalysts often serve as the professional "ego ideal" of psychotherapists, and this is probably as satisfactory a group as can be obtained.

Thus, from a random choice point, every fourth psychoanalyst listed in the 1959–1960 directory of the American Psychoanalytic Association was sent a questionnaire until 300 were mailed. Fifty-three replied (18 per cent), but only 51 questionnaires were available for study. Ordinarily, such a sample would be considered highly inadequate. But it must be remembered that there were only 802 members in the American Psychoanalytic Association at the time, and that the findings represent the attitudes of one out of every 16 members, a significant sampling. It is not known why one psychoanalyst returned his questionnaire and not another. I do know that the decision was apparently not made on the basis of completely favorable attitudes toward the study since many hostile replies were received.

As a control group I used the graduating class, 25 in all, of the Church Divinity School of the Pacific, in Berkeley, California, an Episcopalian training school for ministers. The questionnaire was identical with the one used for the psychoanalysts with the necessary substitutions of "minister" for "psychoanalyst." Ministers of this denomination were selected because they seemed parallel to psychoanalysts socio-economically; because they do pastoral counseling; and because, in general, their concerns are with the existence of people rather than ritual. This particular divinity school draws students from the upper-middle socioeconomic groups; many of its students have left successful careers to go into the ministry.

The average age of the psychoanalysts was fifty-one years (standard error $\pm$ 8.8); the ministers were 34 years old (standard error $\pm$ 9.9). The subjects in both groups were primarily males; there were eight female psychoanalysts and one female minister.[4] Two psychoanalysts and 11 ministers were single. Thus, it can be seen that the ministers are considerably younger and less often married, and fewer of them are women. (This marital difference may in part be due to the age difference.) The ministers were, of course, all Christians; an unknown but probably sizeable percentage of the psychoanalysts were non-Christians. (I did not ask for information about religion.) It should be noted, however, that a Judeo-Christian orientation would probably account for all of the cases. Cappon[5] states that statistically he found that fear of death was independent of type of religion, or the lack of it, of age, and of sex. His study showed, however, a slight tendency for older people to show more overt fear of death than younger people.

Aging apparently predisposes in some way toward more insistent attitudes toward death. There is a 17 year mean age difference between the two groups. This is a substantial difference and may in part account for the differing responses. However, both groups are relatively youthful and I do not know whether an age differentiation of approximately two decades can completely account for the differences in attitude. I am inclined to believe that the structure of thanatophobia is fundamental and not a simple correlative of aging.

The Table summarizes the psychoanalytic and ministerial responses to the questionnaires employing percentages for the open-ended responses which I grossly categorized. In order to make the data easier to grasp, I describe a "typical" psychoanalytic reply,

[4] By canon law the Episcopal church does not ordain women. However, the term "minister," in the sense used here, is satisfactory for her.

[5] Cappon, D. "The Fear of Dying," *Pastoral Psychology*, 1961, *12*, 35–44.

PSYCHOANALYTIC AND MINISTERIAL RESPONSES TO
ITEM-STATEMENTS ON DEATH

| | | Psychoanalysts* | | Ministers | |
|---|---|---|---|---|---|
| 1. | Is death a beginning or an end? | | | | |
| | a. end | 43 | 84.3% | 0 | 0% |
| | b. beginning | 0 | 0 % | 0 | 0% |
| | c. neither | 1 | 2 % | 9 | 36% |
| | d. both | 3 | 5.9% | 14 | 56% |
| | e. don't know | 4 | 7.8% | 0 | 0% |
| | f. other | 0 | 0 % | 2 | 8% |
| 2. | What is the proper time to die?** | | | | |
| | a. old age | 7 | 13.7% | 1 | 4% |
| | b. after completing life's work (reaching goal) | 9 | 17.6% | 1 | 4% |
| | c. when incapacitated ("burden to others") | 16 | 31.4% | 3 | 12% |
| | d. there is none | 11 | 21.6% | 10 | 40% |
| | e. whenever it happens (or "inevitable") | 3 | 5.9% | 4 | 16% |
| | f. other | 8 | 15.7% | 6 | 24% |
| 3. | What is the best way to die?** | | | | |
| | a. painlessly | 9 | 17.6% | 6 | 24% |
| | b. suddenly (quickly) | 18 | 35.3% | 4 | 16% |
| | c. in sleep | 13 | 25.5% | 1 | 4% |
| | d. fully conscious | 2 | 3.9% | 2 | 8% |
| | e. there is none | 1 | 2 % | 4 | 16% |
| | f. fully prepared | 4 | 7.8% | 5 | 20% |
| | g. other | 9 | 17.6% | 8 | 32% |
| | h. natural causes | 6 | 11.8% | 1 | 4% |
| 4. | "The burial ritual is an outmoded personal device." | | | | |
| | a. yes (prefer cremation, giving body to medical school, etc.) | 15 | 29.4% | 1 | 4% |
| | b. no (meets needs of the living, etc.) | 31 | 60.8% | 16 | 64% |
| | c. undecided ("depends on how it's done," culture, etc.) | 5 | 9.8% | 5 | 20% |
| | d. other | 0 | 0 % | 3 | 12% |
| 5. | How many people would miss you were you to die today? (I) How many would you miss were they to die today? (II) | | | | |

|  |  | Psychoanalysts* | | Ministers | |
|---|---|---|---|---|---|
| a. | I > II | 10 | 19.6% | 0 | 0% |
| b. | II < I | 3 | 5.9% | 4 | 16% |
| c. | I = II | 24 | 47.1% | 8 | 32% |
| d. | don't know (or other vague answer) | 14 | 27.5% | 11 | 44% |
| e. | none | 0 | 0 % | 2 | 8% |

6. Ideally, what personal, social, and professional arrangements should be made for one's death?**

|  |  | Psychoanalysts* | | Ministers | |
|---|---|---|---|---|---|
| a. | funeral arrangements | 12 | 23.5% | 12 | 48% |
| b. | care of dependents and insurance | 24 | 47.1% | 11 | 44% |
| c. | disposal of property and will | 8 | 15.7% | 14 | 56% |
| d. | transfer of patients or parishioners | 17 | 33.3% | 2 | 8% |
| e. | disposal of files and records | 6 | 11.8% | 2 | 8% |
| f. | general ("things in order") | 18 | 35.3% | 5 | 20% |
| g. | none | 1 | 2 % | 2 | 8% |
| h. | prepare friends and relatives | 7 | 13.7% | 4 | 16% |
| i. | spiritual preparation | 0 | 0 % | 3 | 12% |

7. "A feeling of immunity toward death is a necessary fiction for psychoanalysts (or ministers)?"

|  |  | Psychoanalysts* | | Ministers | |
|---|---|---|---|---|---|
| a. | no | 41 | 80.4% | 19 | 76% |
| b. | yes | 3 | 5.9% | 1 | 4% |
| c. | sometimes | 1 | 2 % | 2 | 8% |
| d. | other | 6 | 11.8% | 3 | 12% |

8. Should an individual have the right to "choose" his own death?

|  |  | Psychoanalysts* | | Ministers | |
|---|---|---|---|---|---|
| a. | yes | 24 | 47.1% | 0 | 0% |
| b. | no | 7 | 13.7% | 17 | 68% |
| c. | sometimes (incurable cancer, martyrdom, etc.) | 12 | 23.5% | 3 | 12% |
| d. | an impossibility | 2 | 3.9% | 1 | 4% |
| e. | other ("debatable," etc.) | 6 | 11.8% | 4 | 16% |

9. "The inevitability of death assures man of his finiteness and weakness."

112

| | | | | | |
|---|---|---|---|---|---|
| a. | finiteness only | 11 | 21.6% | 4 | 16% |
| b. | weakness only | 0 | 0 % | 0 | 0% |
| c. | both ("true," etc.) | 18 | 35.3% | 12 | 48% |
| d. | neither ("no") | 13 | 25.5% | 3 | 12% |
| e. | "can't answer" (or no answer) "meaningless" | 3 | 5.9% | 2 | 8% |
| f. | other | 6 | 11.8% | 4 | 16% |

10. Do you consider discussions about death best avoided with your patients (or parishioners)?

| | | | | | |
|---|---|---|---|---|---|
| a. | yes | 0 | 0 % | 0 | 0% |
| b. | no | 45 | 88.2% | 24 | 96% |
| c. | sometimes | 5 | 9.8% | 1 | 4% |
| d. | other | 1 | 2 % | 0 | 0% |

\* Percentages are rounded to nearest 0.1.

\*\* Percentages exceed 100 on these items since some subjects gave more than one response.

that is, an abstracted composite of the responses of the psychoanalysts. It must be understood that such an individual does not actually exist and that the "typical" analyst stands at the modal rather than the integrated point of response. This "typical" analyst is called here Dr. Capowitz. Where he is "ambivalent," it is indicated by giving the percentage value of his ambivalence.

Dr. Capowitz believes that death is an end; never is it a beginning (84 per cent).[6] He says, "If you mean do I believe in the myth of the hereafter, I think this is a rather silly question to ask a psychoanalyst. Read Freud's *Future of an Illusion*." However, eight of the 51 psychoanalysts (16 per cent) had reservations and answered, "Don't know," "Both," or "Neither," to the question as to whether "death was a beginning or an end."

Dr. Capowitz believes that the proper time to die is when one's life work is completed, when one is no longer able to function, or when one is a burden to others (63 per cent). He gave this reply: ". . . when a person has little objective chance to become happy,

[6] Percentages as used here mean the per cent of total sample replying in this specific way.

113

to feel that his productions are worthwhile, and when he can no longer produce materials or emotions which contribute to the happiness of others." The distribution of responses to this item shows a wider variation than the first item, possibly because the query was anxiety-producing. Thus, for example, 22 per cent say, "there is no proper time," 16 per cent give a variety of replies, and five per cent, "whenever it happens."

The best way to die is quickly and painlessly, perhaps while asleep (78 per cent). "Preparation" for such an event is helpful (18 per cent), as are "natural causes" (12 per cent) as a way of dying. "Suddenly—and in quick transition—without the biological and spiritual suffering involved in a prolonged separation," our psychoanalyst describes as the best way.

The doctor feels ambivalent about the "function of the burial ritual." In part (30 per cent), he would give it up, because the "psychic work of mourning can be done without it . . . It is an empty and often hypocritical gesture of lip service to a magical and superstitious past." He would just as soon be cremated or would donate his body to a medical school. However, the majority of those questioned (61 per cent) subscribe to the point of view which is subsumed as follows: "I do not agree that the burial ritual is an outmoded device because it is a psychologically valid mechanism applied to society so that the surviving family members of the deceased can elaborate and resolve their grief." "That's the statement of one who would rather avoid the reality of dying. I hear it from those whose lives are felt by themselves to be meaningless."

Our psychoanalyst had difficulty determining how many people would miss him after death, and how many he would miss. He believes the proportion would be about equal: He would miss the same quantum who would miss him. Conjectures ranged numerically from three to 300. Where the number was large, it usually included his patients; where it was small, only family members were involved. In general, however, his belief is that he will be missed more than he will miss others.

In anticipating his death, Dr. Capowitz's primary concern

is for the care of his dependents (47 per cent). Next, he would "generally" get things in order (35 per cent). Concern for the transference of his patients to another analyst follows (33 per cent). He is only moderately interested in funeral arrangements (24 per cent), and still less (14 per cent) in anticipatory preparation of his friends and more distant relatives for his death; the disposal of his files and records is of minor concern (12 per cent).

He does not subscribe to the statement that "a feeling of immunity toward death is a necessary fiction" (80 per cent). Rather, he prefers "a reality-oriented consideration in which death is not considered as some loss of identity, separation anxiety, or what have you, but a statistical certainty which will come in due time." Only 6 per cent will admit that such a fiction does in fact operate, or may be necessary.

He feels most often that an individual does have the right to choose his own death (47 per cent), particularly under such unique conditions as incurable cancer, heroism, martyrdom, and so on (24 per cent additional to above). Nine (18 per cent) say "no," or "impossible"; six more (12 per cent) consider choice debatable.

Faced with the inevitability of death, he again is ambivalent as to whether "death assures him of his finiteness and weakness" and says, "No, it does not. It does this only for the very immature and poorly evolved personality, when the 'death concept' may become the repository by projection of his anxieties that derive from poor maturation" (26 per cent). In regard to finitude, he says "Yes, only for one who dares think it and can accept it" (57 per cent).

When asked if a discussion of death is best avoided in the analysis of the patient, he almost completely disagrees (88 per cent). Only five psychoanalysts (10 per cent) think such discussion should "sometimes" be avoided. Interestingly enough, he thinks that this presents no problem since "the subject rarely arises." He says, "Of course these matters always end up in the areas of aggression, castration anxiety, or a mystical union (desexualized) with an idealized figure."

115

If the "about-to-be-ordained" minister, whom I call Mr. Caldwell, is considered in the same "typical" fashion, this is what is found. Mr. Caldwell does not believe that death is either an end or a beginning. For him death marks a point in the linear existence of that identity which we call "self." "The continuation 'or beginning' of life after death to me is actually that aspect of true living which we have experienced in life through faith in God and living relationships with Him." It is thus both "a beginning and an end" (56 per cent), and "neither a beginning or end" (36 per cent). The question itself is a disorderly one for the ministers.

In light of the above, "the proper time to die" is almost irrelevant, for he says, "There's no proper time for physical death—one dies when one dies" (64 per cent). Yet, he also wants to die "painlessly" (24 per cent), "fully prepared" (20 per cent), and "quickly" (16 per cent). Mr. Caldwell says, "The best way to die is with as little pain as possible, with as much preparation of family and friends as is foreseeable, and in the hope that one has lived a life in response to God through compassionate response to others."

In contrast to the psychoanalyst, the minister does not believe that burial rituals are outmoded (64 per cent). "The Christian burial is an attempt to witness to the fact of the reality of death on the one hand, and the nonfinality of it on the other. It is a declaration by the Christian community that Christians have nothing to fear from death because one can never pass outside of God's loving concern." Mr. Caldwell would be missed by fewer people than he would miss, but this may be due to the fact that none of the ministers had as yet been assigned a parish. In general, the quantum was small, usually including only "family and close friends."

Like Dr. Capowitz, in preparing for his death Mr. Caldwell would arrange for the disposal of his property (56 per cent), make necessary funeral arrangements (48 per cent), and arrange for the care of his dependents (44 per cent).

He does not believe that an individual has the right to "choose his own death" (72 per cent), but allows that there are

116

situations (28 per cent) in which such a stricture might have to be tempered. He believes, at any rate, "that it is not Christian teaching that he have the right to choose his own death since his life itself was given to him by God—and its earthly close is likewise in God's hands."

Mr. Caldwell agrees more than does Dr. Capowitz (57 per cent) that "the inevitability of death assures man of his finiteness and weakness." "This is a true statement, as I understand it, and a theologically significant one. It is precisely this finiteness and weakness that shows man that he is not God . . ." He feels that discussions of death should be encouraged rather than avoided (88 per cent), and 10 per cent more have only slight reservations about discussing it. His reason is, "How else can we help them live life in the proper perspective?"

Our findings may be stated as follows. Death is so compelling an idea that man has always required some irrationality and magic to handle his feelings about it. In his long history only the forms of defense toward death have changed. If one considers individually the responses of the psychoanalysts to the questionnaire, one must conclude that psychoanalysts also defend themselves against death. The uniformity, certainty, brevity, and frequent hostility of the respondents' statements, in an area where uncertainty and diversity are the norm, makes one suspect the operation of defenses rather deeply anchored. These defenses I would like to consider in terms of denial, displacement, and compensation.

*Denial.* The fact that psychoanalysts feel so uniformly that the discussion of death should not be avoided in psychoanalysis, but indicate that it rarely comes up, is in itself a denial of the phenomenon of death. The experience of psychotherapists at large is that, if allowed, it is introduced in various forms. The patient soon learns from subtle countertransference attitudes what can and what cannot safely be brought up in the hour, what makes the psychotherapist comfortable and what makes him uncomfortable. The possibility of death for the psychotherapist (vacations, illness, professional meetings), and for himself, is a recurring thought of the patient; placing it on the open agenda, however, has all manner of resistances connected with it. Now, of course, the psychotherapist has no open stricture against discussing death, or any other topic for that matter. But his denial may be of such a subtle nature that both he and the patient are unaware of it. Suppose, for example, that thanatophobia is always analyzed or reduced to a lower denominator, such as castration anxiety, so that it can never stand as a reality in its own right. This would of itself constitute a form of denial of the absolute fact that the therapist and the patient will die, and that they may at the present moment be afraid of death. The selection of "what to talk about" in psychotherapy is not always as random as therapists want to believe, for patients speak of what the therapist wants or needs to hear.

Death is an existential fact, and possibly the prototype of all human separations. But invariably to interpret thanatophobia as castration or separation anxiety, or the need for an idealized union with a symbolic "other," is to substitute historicity when contemporaneity or futurity is indicated. Certainly the trauma of separation in the history of the individual sets the tone for the ultimate one, but it is a mistake to force death into a single mold and thus constrain the entire treatment situation. There is no reason why one should not feel anxious about leaving a life he finds rewarding and irreplaceable. The Judeo-Christian sense of sin also adds to the anxiety by the future promise of punishment or reward. This issue must be faced as a reality situation where analyzing it may actually deny it. The analysis of thanatophobia contributes to its reconstruction as a living force, and to the recognition of a life process which transcends both birth and death in life. I have often wondered why it was that classical psychoanalysis shied away from the psychoanalysis of people in the final reaches of life, and the explanation that youth is where the libido primarily manifests itself (in conflict) does not satisfy me. The countertransferences which come with a succession of mature patients who fear Thanatos can be too much

118

for analysts to bear. The present study would seem to offer some evidence that ministers encourage discussions of death with their parishioners because they are more comfortable with its implications, whereas psychoanalysts tend to discourage it by subverting it dynamically.

Each humanistic profession has a necessary mythology which permits it to get on with the disagreeable aspects of its work. This is as true for theology as it is for psychotherapy. These myths are, in a sense, necessary and convenient fictions which serve not only the good of the practitioner but the patient or parishioners as well. Such myths permit the operation of a social process which indeed has no convincing rationale if examined in the light of scientific objectivity. Some such mechanism must operate in the case of people who constantly place their lives in jeopardy in occupational and recreational forms. The driver of a racing car at Le Mans must believe that he has, at least for this event, an immunity from death, and the man giving the San Francisco Golden Gate Bridge a coat of paint must feel similarly. But all people have such fictions, and because of them life goes more smoothly. Not to admit that one does at times subscribe to such fictions is to use the mechanism of denial.

*Displacement.* Thanatophobia can also be displaced, and its anxious content thereby removed; thus, in psychotherapy, Thanatos can be displaced upon Eros. It was only when Freud's constructs about the human personality had reached a highly developed stage that he realized that Eros was not sufficient. He then added Thanatos in opposition to but in conjunction with Eros. Jung had independently and somewhat earlier come to a similar conclusion. Much time and effort in classical psychoanalysis are given over to analyzing the libido and its vicissitudes and, in fact, it has only been since the recent refurbishing of ego psychology that the libido has assumed what is perhaps a more proper place. I would say, in part, that the overwhelming emphasis on the passionate, pleasurable, and sexual aspects of the human being is a displacement of that aspect which

119

rightly belongs to the mature, individuated, and declining organism. As Weigert explains it,[7] "The exclusion of death deprives life of its meaning, the personality of its wholeness, and human relations of the depth of mutuality." The image of ourselves we want to see is that of the youthful, vigorous persons we treat, instinctual and enduring. Through them we may unconsciously displace and obviate our own decline.

The displacement of Thanatos adds to Eros' already precarious burden. Such displacement by the psychotherapist simply mirrors what culture itself displaces in its fear. Life becomes motoric rather than contemplative, object-oriented rather than inner-oriented, and everywhere a shallow Eros abounds. Psychotherapy falls into a trap, for the analysis of passion is itself a form of passion. The displacement of the possibilities of death deprives the individual of the possibilities of freedom, for, as Camus says, "The only possible freedom is a freedom with respect to death. The truly free man is he who, accepting death as such, at the same time accepts its consequences—that is, the reversal of all life's traditional values."[8] Psychotherapy is, if anything, itself a call to freedom.

*Compensation.* Compensation as a mechanism supervenes for a felt but not necessarily verbalized deficiency. To feel weak and finite when one wants to be strong and infinite calls for compensative adjustments. This is a well-known principle and its dynamism requires no elaboration. If one fears death, life becomes that much sweeter in order to compensate for something that one will reluctantly have to terminate. Compensation for something completely unknown comes to have a special free-floating quality or yearning which is never sated. It produces a life-upon-life with a sense of terrible urgency, and time becomes dislocated into the essence of life rather than its epiphenomenon. The moment-for-itself becomes difficult. Death, in this way, makes no creative contribution to the

[7] Weigert, E. "The Nature of Sympathy in the Art of Psychotherapy." *Psychiatry,* 1961, *24,* 187–196.
[8] Camus, A. "From a Writer's Notebook." *Encounter,* 1961, *17 No. 4,* 19.

living but torments the individual with an unseen burden. The ego under such circumstances tends to organize its data in an imperative way which gives existence an appearance of still photographs rather than a montage.

Such compensation in the humanistic professions often results in a "search" which may itself be a negation of the person inside.[9] The minister is better compensated by his dogma and ritual than the psychoanalyst, and there is, I feel, more acceptance of death and less inhibition of the topic with his parishioners. Since he does not believe that death is an end, he can rationalize the continuity of this existence with something to come later. This quiets his anxiety about finitude. But, more important, he has his divinity in a unique way while the psychoanalyst usually has no divine source.[10] The dynamics of a Supreme Father (or Mother) in allaying anxiety are now sufficiently understood. Whether they are mythological or realistic, their effects can be and often are similar. Mythology has a considerable tradition in the religious history of man, whereas formalized therapeutic procedures are indeed youthful. This is not to advocate mythologies or fictions in life but to point up their social and personal effects. The way of scientists is the way of reality, and that is why the unconscious must be made conscious.[11]

If, then, one does not gain invincibility by religious means, one must obtain it from one's inner self. Such a fiction of invincibility, as I have pointed out, may be a temporary desideratum of existence. Anxious patients are noteworthy for the breakdown in their feelings of invincibility. The fact that they have come to psy-

[9] See, for example, Wheelis, A. *The Seeker.* New York: Random House, 1960; and *The Quest for Identity.* New York: Norton, 1958.

[10] It has been suggested that this is one explanation for the frequent deification of Sigmund Freud by his disciples.

[11] It is interesting to speculate: If one were in the final moments of dying, and all had been done medically that could be done, would one call for a priest or psychotherapist? I would like to think that the psychotherapist would receive the call, but I doubt that he would. The possible reasons for this are interesting in their own right, but they would represent society's appreciation of the inadequacy of psychotherapists in this special situation.

121

chotherapy at all may be related to the wish to be closer to the "invincible one," and they give up psychotherapy only when they again feel somewhat invincible. Symbolic death may be for them just that absence of the quality of invincibility which is possibly the feeling of castration itself. The history of theology shows that great theologians of the past, such as Martin Luther, felt invincible only when they opposed the Devil. Beyond that, they were self-effacing and unsure men who lived through resignation in the face of God. If we equate the Unconscious for the moment with the Devil, then psychotherapists need a continuous infusion of invincibility, since they are constantly jousting with the Unconscious.

The need to feel invincible brings its own penalties, however, for not only must the myth of invincibility be maintained at the cost of considerable energy, but it inhibits a true encounter between the two people in psychotherapy. It permits one to assume a privileged, but invalid, position in the face of humanity, which is detrimental in the relationship. Of course, it is necessary to maintain a position of authority and prestige with patients, and this is a fundamental aspect of the transference situation. Nevertheless, there is an increasing acceptance of the philosophy which says that a true encounter can only take place when patient and psychotherapist meet each other on an I-Thou basis. In such a relationship there is no room for privilege.

Nowhere is the feeling of invincibility so manifestly a deterrent as in the psychotherapy of schizophrenic patients. These patients find extreme difficulty in entering a therapeutic relationship at all, in part because they fear the double-binding properties of their significant past relationships. Their binding involved an "invincible one" in the past, and they were in a way seduced by a promise of love which carried too great a penalty. Their reluctance is therefore understandable. As I will show, the kind of psychotherapy which seems to work best with them is a mutual encounter on deep symbolic levels. Furthermore, schizophrenic patients are peculiarly occupied with delusions of death and rebirth, and the process of their recovery often seems an analogous form of resurrection. These preoccupations are apparent not only in their manifest behavioral content but in all sorts of fantasies. If the psychotherapist is made uncomfortable by the symbolic death and rebirth, he will tend to diminish its importance or substitute for it. The patient will not in essence be permitted to make the choice between life and death. The choice for freedom is the patient's philosophical decision to make, and he must feel that it is his own decision. In this regard the sensitivity of psychotherapists to death is noted by the fact that the suicide of a patient in private or public practice is met with a great sense of shame and guilt. Yet the public understands that suicide is a recognizable hazard of this particular profession. It must then be the unconscious which troubles therapists who cannot face the possibility of a choice of suicide on the part of the patient.

It would be important to know how the unconscious of psychotherapists and ministers perceives death. I do not agree with Freud's statement that the unconscious does not know of it. The unconscious is the repository of all that is symbolic of life and death, and it is the font of creativity. Creation contains destruction, and the unconscious is the residual of death and all that is archaic. Ultimately, the consciousness to which we cling becomes the total unconscious. What we really fear on the deepest of levels is, then, in the unconscious, and the fear of the primary process may be the fear of the components of death. If there is a death instinct, its repression involves maintaining it intact and unsullied in the unconscious. But, as we have seen, existence involves both Eros and Thanatos, and to diminish one for the benefit of the other is to deny what life holds. To stop short in making this part of the unconscious conscious is to vitiate the maxims by which therapy is practiced.

The psychoanalysts who were studied indicate that they would prefer to die suddenly, painlessly, or in their sleep. Ministers feel this way too and on a rational basis this is understandable. For example, the "hero" in society becomes a "hero" by facing death under circumstances which are not typical or usual. He sacrifices something irreplaceable for a "goal" when few can or will make that sacrifice. In this way he resolves, reinstates, and transcends himself, and his death makes him heroic. It may be valuable to consider the "hero" in culture an archetype, since he has been present in every culture and in the residuals of men's minds. Usually, the "hero" does not die painlessly and suddenly, and certainly never in bed, but, rather, lingeringly and with deep suffering. Because of his suffering, the hero's death is dynamically shared by all men. Each shares in his transcendence and rises above his own mundane, effortless, unheroic death.

Death as it is portrayed in literature and drama is the central focus of human action. Hemingway, who was notoriously preoccupied with death in his novels, brought sudden, violent, and often transfiguring deaths to his heroes. They are on the psychoanalytic model in that they are quickly over. But the Greek tragedies of Sophocles, Aeschylus and Euripides, and the *Phaedo* of Plato,[12] provide for a different model which is similar to the pattern accepted during the Middle Ages. Death in these periods was conceived as a prolonged, often transcending, psychic suffering, accompanied by mortification of the body. The process provided for some kind of continuity either by ascensionism, by a descent to regions below, or with the minds of later men. Seldom is death seen by culture as the end. Thus, if literature and drama mirror the needs of culture and individuals, death as an end (painless and quick) is a relatively recent development which is supplanting the classical position. The American Western movie invariably has the villain instantly shot dead, which reflects the comfortable termination the aggressor and victim both want.

The important point is that thanatophobia in its repressive aspects calls for an unreconstructed psychic sacrifice in the living. This need not occur, if only life and death can be seen as biological and psychological polarities of existence without mythologies or fictions of any kind.

---

[12] Socrates was reconciled to his death, and even sought it. But he had to wait a month before he could die, until the ship commemorating Theseus' voyage to Crete returned from Delos. Plato also describes the actual death—growing coldness—of Socrates' body in a slow and lingering way.

# PART III

---

## TREATMENT STUDIES

# CHAPTER 11

# Tess: Flight from Caritas

The typescripts of the psychotherapeutic interviews with Tess include a great quantity of material. My past experience with schizophrenics has been that no report can reproduce the qualitative essence of the interaction and that one has to be reconciled to an abstracted, if not distorted, representation. Thus I will make no attempt to reproduce the course of the psychotherapy in what follows, but will instead discuss certain phases of the treatment. The patient was first seen for thirty hours of group therapy, and then had eighty-six hours of individual therapy as a resident patient and an outpatient from April 15, 1956, to July 1, 1958. She was twenty-eight years old at the time of admission. Just prior to July 1, 1958, she was followed by a psychiatric social worker in connection with post-hospital adjustment. No report will be given here of the latter work or of the group therapy.

Before I discuss the treatment proper, a synopsis of the life history is offered.

As far as is known, Tess first came to the attention of a psycho-analyst in September 1948. She was unkempt, confused, and somewhat depressed. There was a concerned, philosophical tone to her mental content, and she was preoccupied with sexual fantasies about her father. Death, rape, and sex were recurrent themes in her mentation. After a brief period of treatment she became paranoid, believing that the FBI was following her. She said she wanted complete gratification or to be extinguished. Following this, she remitted her symptoms in a few months, but suffered a second psychotic episode late in 1949.

Again she improved rapidly and was in good enough condition to marry in 1951. She moved to another part of the United States, 3000 miles away, with her husband and suffered further breakdowns necessitating outpatient psychiatric treatment. She returned to the original city in 1955, having separated from her husband, and resumed treatment with her original psychoanalyst. At this time her defenses were severely decompensated, and she complicated her condition by drinking to reduce tensions. It became necessary to hospitalize her in a private sanitarium in November and December 1955, where she improved rapidly. However, she was not capable of handling her environment and was referred to the state hospital where I saw her.

Upon admission Tess told the psychiatrist that her emotional difficulties were chronologically related to the time her father fell ill. (He subsequently died of his illness.) She had fantasies that her parents were not her real ones. She bordered on the delusion that she was the daughter of the famous artist Picasso, but at the same time was able to be critical of the delusion. She said that she was unstable and uncertain about her future, and that she could not control the impulse to escape conflict by drinking. The psychiatrist described her as "oriented, relevant, mildly depressed, but revealing a great deal of anxiety and instability if left unprotected." She adjusted well to ward routine. Because of her talent in art she was assigned to the art section in the occupational therapy department. Her designs were quite creative but she tended to be intense, and worked slowly and cautiously.

About two months after admission she surreptitiously obtained some form of stimulant, possibly alcohol, and apparently threw herself in front of an oncoming car, but without causing damage to herself. It was not clear whether the intent was self-destruction. Again she improved, and asked to leave. Since she was a voluntary patient, and the

128

improvement seemed general, permission was granted in May 1956. Diagnosis was schizophrenic reaction, chronic undifferentiated type, although a neurosis and character disorder had been considered.

Tess returned, however, in just six days and told a strange story. She said that she had started to drink again, that she was raped in a bar, and that she wanted to drown herself but could not. She was depressed and vague, but oriented and without delusions. Her ward psychiatrist at this time mentioned pseudo-neurotic schizophrenia with acting-out. At this time we agreed that she would discontinue group therapy with me and that I would see her individually. After fifteen hours of individual therapy she became increasingly tense, tearful, and depressed. She was considered acutely psychotic and transferred to a ward where maximum supervision was afforded. She lost considerable weight. Reserpine (two mg. a day) was administered by the ward psychiatrist and, when this was ineffective, electric-convulsive therapy was started. The patient was now actively delusional, withdrawn, confused, and depressed.

She showed marked improvement with six ECT and was no longer delusional or depressed. She returned to an open ward. Psychotherapy was continuous during this time, varying from the initial two hours a week to four hours as the circumstances dictated. A month later she had two extended visits to her mother and then became delusional again. This was a brief psychotic period which the patient gave up by working through basic conflicts in the psychotherapy. In February 1957, she obtained employment in the book department of a large department store and left the hospital. She continued to come in for psychotherapy as an outpatient until I left for another part of the state.

Tess is the younger of two siblings, both girls. She is a little more than twenty months the junior of her sister who is happily married to a college professor and has several children. Her sister had been in analysis and had been helped by it. Tess's father was born in Puerto Rico and was the export manager for a large U. S. company. He was full of energy and ambition but suffered from stomach trouble. The father and mother were reportedly happy early in the marriage. Later he was attracted to other women and many years of discord followed. The father was apparently a seductive person in his relationship to his daughters and needed the adoration of women. The mother, whom I

129

never met, is reported as a nongiving person, but has been described on short acquaintance as pleasant, intelligent, and charming. She was born in the Middle West and has been troubled with a chronic duodenal ulcer and a heart complaint. Her father was an alcoholic and her mother committed suicide.

The patient was educated in Cuba, at a private school, and came to the United States at age eleven. She was a very bright girl and graduated from high school at sixteen. Her achievement was reduced, however, because of persistent headaches and an illness of undescribed origin. She obtained a scholarship to an art school which she attended for a time.

In 1951 she married the son of an artist of considerable renown. The husband, a Ph.D., was a scientist who later came into some stature in his own right. The patient considers him cold, unresponsive, and perfectionistic, but he seemed genuinely interested in her welfare. Tess said that he was a good provider, and that their sexual adjustment was initially good but later deteriorated.

"I just drank too much starting after a miscarriage in 1952. I was extremely depressed. . . . We agreed intellectually and philosophically. But he was overly critical of me in order to boost himself up. He needed to show me off rather than to have me for himself. He had a compulsion to go skiing and tried to make a skier of me, but I was afraid."

There was no issue from the marriage. They were divorced after four and a half years, but were together for only a part of this time.

The mother described Tess in her younger days as a "delightful person, charming, sweet, like a balm. She is gentle and soft-spoken. She is easy to make friends with and everyone appears to like her." The patient had difficulty in learning to read and complained frequently of headaches. Glasses were obtained for her. She would have frequent "acidosis" and stay home from school. Her sister was exemplary in school and attained some prominence at the university she attended. A considerable rivalry was established and Tess always felt that her mother favored her sister under the pretext of her sister's nervousness.

Tess was very idealistic and had difficulty choosing a husband, although she had many admirers. The patient was encouraged in her art ability but wanted to start at the top. She could not work consistently and painstakingly. At twenty-one, when her father died, Tess showed the first flowering of her psychopathology. She was depressed for three months and inactivated in bed. She seemed to recover but became psychotic in Europe where her mother took her for a change of scene.

Both girls were largely raised by a Cuban nurse who was faithful to the family and stayed with them until her death. Tess was her favorite. She is described by Tess as "having a lot of common sense, a lot of warmth, very religious, a fine person," and she called her Caridad.

Tess became the focus of my attention as one of seven women who participated with me twice weekly in group therapy on the hospital admission ward. She was small, almost petite, in structure, with brown hair not distinguished in any way. Her complexion was on the pale side, but her features were classic. She spoke quietly although with distinction. There was a tendency to measure her words, but she did not talk in the clipped speech of the frightened who hold back. She was obviously quite bright and her factual information on aesthetics, travel, history, and similar matters distinguished her from the other members of the group. She had a quality of intensity, or sincerity, and a sense of purpose which brooked no compromise. She wanted to get well, knew the costs, and wanted to settle them. Every psychotherapist of schizophrenia is challenged by the suffering and struggles of such patients, and each of us unconsciously introjects certain of these patients and attempts to bring them to the treatment relationship.

After a number of hours of group therapy I offered Tess the opportunity of seeing me individually. She was reluctant and made some semi-objective references in which she deprecated me in comparison with her former analyst, who practiced nearby. Her criticism continued even after she accepted treatment from me and is important dynamically in its own right. She came two to four hours a week; the frequency was consistent from week to week but varied sometimes with the needs of the patient. Thus, when she became overtly delusional, I saw her four hours a week; when her delusions passed over, we returned to two or three hours. In this way I ma-

131

nipulated our presence together for support and independent action, honored special requests to see me, and often went to her ward to see her when she was disturbed. This was particularly true in the earlier stages of treatment. Acting-out and suicidal attempts, mock or otherwise, were taken as a matter of course and were made the focus of examination, subject to proper therapeutic timing. She was very much afraid of her drinking propensities but still would rather have "passed" as an alcoholic. I did not accept her excuse and considered her drinking as a screen.

The vicissitudes of the therapy were always buttressed by our encounter, and by the knowledge, conscious and unconscious, that we were together in this great struggle of hers. She tested our relationship in many ways: by silence, aggression, absence, mania, depression, overdetermined affection, suicidal attempt, returning to her psychoanalyst, and so on. The basic commitment never varied. As a rule I handle the patients' aggressions much better than I do their love. I found that not only was more love required than I was prepared to give, but that later, when I gave it, I became anxious and guilty about my feelings. This limited the therapy to a plateau for several weeks until I successfully resolved the countertransference.

Conventionally, the progress of the psychotherapy involved the development of the transference and countertransference, and their resolution. This is an elementary fact of treatment which masks more basic and dynamic factors. Sechehaye sees the problem of schizophrenia as an oral one and the therapy as compensatory on this level. I would agree that the treatment involves this but that it is not limited to it. One is also impressed with the anal and Oedipal trauma encountered. This was certainly true in Tess's case. Psychotherapy, then, according to our formulation, involves the "undoing" and "redoing" of all the levels through encounters. This is, in essence, the process of growth which psychotherapy makes possible.

The encounter operates on the various developmental levels; unfortunately, there is little objective information about what happens in a significant encounter. The literature on the oral phases is now well documented and one can be referred to Sechehaye[1] among others. About the Oedipal period we also have some facts, but less is known of the anal and genital levels. We know that the encounter occurs and we can see its effects. It is the source of behavioral pathology, as well as the basis for the cure. *The schizophrenic redoes and reintegrates his trauma through the meaning of symbols and the acting-out of symbolic material;* and the encounter becomes the highest point of symbolization in the patient's treatment. This was patently true for Tess. The symbolic value of black–white, the Virgin Mary, father, and rape in her case will be discussed.

At some point in the psychotherapy the schizophrenic has the choice of giving up her own fantasies for the reality of the here-now and her other being for the being she really is. The following fragment from an interview with Tess fairly late in the psychotherapy is illustrative. The patient had again become psychotic and had to be returned to a closed ward. More tranquilizers and electric-convulsive treatment were being considered by her ward psychiatrist. The situation seemed such that we feared all of our work would be undone. It was therefore necessary to confront her with her choice: to evade the encounter by being psychotic or to accept its meaning. The therapy had been a prelude to this point in her life and, while there was considerable danger in such a confrontation, we thought that she had the necessary ego-strength. T represents the patient, and B the therapist:

B: You were starting to say I—I did something?
T: I—sort of have a feeling that you forced some of it.
B: Oh. By what I did or what I am as a person?
T: By, in a sense, . . . uh . . . you're telling me "Listen you're just going around and about, now let's get to the point." And then I felt (*pause*) this—if I went on going around I'd never get to the

[1] Sechehaye, M. A. "La Réalisation symbolique, un catalipeur de la structuration du Moi Schizophrenique." Bâle: Karger, 1957. *A New Psychotherapy in Schizophrenia: Relief of Frustration by Symbolic Realization.* New York: Grune & Stratton, 1956. "The Transference in Symbolic Realization." *International Journal of Psychoanalysis,* 1956, *37,* 270–277; and others.

point and I'd never get well. Or—and that you would not continue therapy.

B: The fear of losing me?

T: That—that was pretty strong.

B: But I never threatened you.

T: No, I know. I don't know what it was. But I know I had that feeling.

B: Maybe you had another feeling too. (*Pause.*) A feeling of relationship with me.

T: Yes, I did—very strongly I remember until . . . uh . . . at one point when—remember when I felt that you were accusing me of terrible crimes and ———.

B: Hm-m.

T: At this point . . . uh . . . it sort of went around and I (*buzzer*) you became in a sense the opposite—an enemy, not as a friend.

B: At that time I was an enemy.

T: Yes, I felt very strongly that you didn't—you didn't like me and you were somehow . . . uh . . . it was like a trap that . . . uh . . . well that you were going to hand me over to the authorities and so on if I told you anything about my ——— associations and all these other crimes. But in a way I think that maybe you're saying well, you're—there was something about—I don't know if it was the tone of your voice or what and maybe I . . . uh . . . associated it with my father. Uh . . . it was a little bit like—as though if I had told him a lie and he was aware of it and he was forcing me to say that I had and that if I didn't say that there would be punishment or even if I did say that there would be punishment anyway. I don't know, it's something (*pause*) I guess a little as though you had become authoritarian and . . . uh . . . (*pause*) and a little as though you were treating me like a child. I . . . uh . . . now stop wandering around and come to the point (*laugh*).

B: Hm-m.

T: And— (*pause*).

B: But you wanted to be a child then (*pause*). Your psychosis represented that (*pause*). And remember I put it to you either you take your psychosis or you take reality. It was up to you.

T: Un-huh (*pause*). Yes. Well, it was that. It was sort of (*pause*) putting it like that and the . . . uh . . . (*long pause and sigh*) I can't—well, I'll try. It was as though you were . . . uh . . . you could have suddenly become my parents and they were saying you have to grow up and be responsible or you have to go away and find your way somehow (*very long pause*). And maybe I wanted to be a child, yet I have the feeling that I resented this treatment. Uh . . . (*pause*) ——— way for treating children (*mutual laughter*).

B: Was it after this that you felt I was against you? Going to punish you for being a criminal?

T: Un-huh.

B: After that, huh?

T: Uh-huh. It began I think around then—well around that time, maybe a little earlier. I had this feeling . . .

B: You were ———.

T: Sort of getting discouraged with me now and . . . uh, uh . . . that this was sort of like a last resort and if I didn't respond then that was it. And . . .

B: I remember being discouraged at that time.

T: Well, I could feel it (*pause*).

B: But discouraged not at you. At both of us that we hadn't been able to work it out. You were again psychotic.

T (*pause*): I think this is a little bit when I began to feel and feel a little more clearly that this—psychosis; though that prior to it that we had begun to establish good relations and to be working fairly well until it became a little more difficult and then that the psychosis is like a way of getting away. Almost as though I could hardly live without psychosis to carry me through.

B: Hm-m.

Earlier the idea of omnipotence in schizophrenia was introduced. I said then that the schizophrenic is preoccupied with life and death, and with his own power over life and death. In close relationships schizophrenics want to destroy the self and others, and to find rebirth. In a paradoxical way they believe that their psychosis permits another to live, and that if they were to give up being schizophrenic someone else might die. This was the ever-present

135

symbolic potential with one or another of their parents, and so it is now with the psychotherapist. With Tess omnipotence was present in three different aspects. In the first, she told about a terrible childhood feeling of omnipotence over ants, and of her control of the world through peopled ants.

T: It was like . . . uh . . . flat I suppose, second story flat, and in the back was the porch (*pause*). It wasn't covered over and the sun beat down on it and I used to go out there and play. And . . . uh . . . (*sigh*) playing was lying on my stomach and—and having a—a tray of water and collecting ants and killing them or maiming them and dumping them in the water to see how long it would take them to come back to life and how . . . uh . . . torture. And thinking during that time, oh, about God and why we're here and also feeling sort of supernatural as though I was in contact with some sort of supernatural cosmic mind or something (*pause*). But I guess I—I'd feel very powerful because I could do this to those little ants—kill them, torture them (*long pause*). And I guess maybe I was thinking of these—I was probably (*pause*) saying this ant is so and so and this other ant is so and so. I'm going to do this and that to it.

B: You mean you identified them?

T: I don't remember actually doing it too clear, a little hazy feeling that I did. Maybe it's too horrible for me to think that I could do such a thing (*long pause*). And I remember another time I was —it was in the afternoon and I was lying on my bed and I was having a fantasy. And the fantasy was where I—as if I was like God and I was going to—this was my world. I had a whole world that belonged—and I was going to tell everybody what to do and control them. Like little dolls in miniature and all these people were little miniatures and I was enormous and could force them to do whatever I wanted. And the fantasy of what I wanted them to do was that they were all going to have a room of their own and there was going to be a man and a woman in each room and they were all going to have sexual intercourse. And I was going to force them.

B: You would manipulate them till they would?

T: In some magical way. Sort of like those ants had grown into more distinctive creatures (*pause*). I felt really that I was omnipotent or (*pause*) I remember thinking so strongly that if I weren't living, if I—almost if I died or I wasn't there, the world wouldn't exist which is true in a way it wouldn't for me . . . And this (*pause*) so from there I went to thinking well the world then and everything exists only because I'm here to perceive it. Which has some truth in it too. For any of us it does, if we're not living or here. . . .

B: We perceive the world through our own senses.

T: Otherwise— Yes, if we are dead, then we don't . . . uh . . . (*pause*). But I had it so much more involved in the way that (*pause*) I had the feeling that I was almost like in contact with God. I was special, special messenger or sometimes (*pause*) . . .

In the second fragment the patient brings up the association of the Virgin Mary in her discussion about the social worker she is seeing.

T: And not as someone always to criticize and tell what to do . . . uh . . . (*long pause*). And in a sense who I feel is older and more mature, someone that I sort of look up to and sort of like an ideal. I, well, like a mother figure, I guess—supposed to be. The Virgin Mary (*laugh*).

B: The Virgin Mary?

T: I do a lot of thinking about the ideal woman and how the Virgin Mary is the ideal woman to a lot of women.

B: To you?

T: No.

B: Well, you mentioned her.

T: Maybe deeply, unconsciously she is. I—

B: You see Miss ———— as . . .

T: No, I . . .

B: As an analogy there?

T: No, not as—I don't see her as the Virgin Mary.

B: No, but as an analogy.

T: As an ideal. Yes, somehow.

B: Hm-m.

T: Or (*pause*) well, she— I would like to be more like her, say, than I would like to be like my mother. I don't want to be like my mother (*pause*). And I don't want to be exactly like Miss ———— either but . . . uh . . . there's more in her that I would like to be like (*long pause*).

B: It is rather interesting that of all the women in history you might have picked, you picked the Virgin Mary.

T: Well, I think she was—she would be the one that Caridad[2] always selected. It was her ideal woman and I think she had her all confused with her mother. She feels that the Virgin Mary is her mother in heaven. She lost her mother when she was two or three days old or something. And she always—she had pictures of the Virgin Mary all over her room and she would always point her out to me as the mother and maybe I associated her with my own mother . . . as far as actual close motherly feelings I always felt Caridad supplied this. My mother was distant. Uh . . . (*pause*) I used to see her once in a while. Well, she never fed me or clothed me or did anything like this. It was always Caridad. And Caridad always told me that I should in a sense have sort of reverence for my mother that one has for the Virgin Mary (*long pause and sigh*). There's a lot going through my mind and I can't seem to get it out.

Not only is Tess omnipotent but she controls through procreation and death. This is why her own sexuality had overtones not only of creation but of dying. The Virgin Mary represents first her mother, and thus her own, that is, Tess's, immaculate conception and also her (Tess's) saintliness. But since she is also her mother,[3] she is the Virgin Mary. It is significant that Tess first became overtly psychotic when her father died. Her omnipotent and incestuous wishes were, in fantasy, construed as having caused his death, and she needed to give him rebirth. In therapy these fantasies and

---

[2] The servant who took care of Tess.

[3] A social worker who interviewed the mother at length was struck by the physical and psychological likeness of the two.

138

wishes, along with others, were worked through so that the need for all power was no longer necessary.

The aspect of masculinity-femininity in Tess is best portrayed by a series of drawings she did. Because the communication aspect involved in the treatment was so poor, I asked Tess at the beginning of each hour to "draw a person" and at the end of the hour to "draw the therapist." I left the room when she did this to allow her fantasies some play and to avoid portrayal effects. I wanted in this non-verbal way to understand the transference and her self-projections better. It was apparent that not only did her self lack definition but there was a masculinity-femininity confusion: many of the drawings were male and female. As treatment continued this bipolarity disappeared and sexual definition was better established. In the final stages the "draw a person," the first drawings made at each session, were highly feminine and receptive. Not long after this improvement she consummated a relationship with a man, married him, and bore a child. Nine years after treatment, she is functioning capably and has not returned to the hospital.

The ethical sense in schizophrenia is related to the basis of all interpersonal relationships, to that process of identification and introjection which makes a sensitive human society possible. I have already said that love is the foundation of the ethical sense and that without it there can be no basis or motives for intimate human relationships. The earliest years are crucial in developing the ability to give and receive love and in establishing basic trust. The pattern for love is set by those adults who, having conceived and produced, expect love from their offspring. But in order to make love possible in the children, the parents must be capable of it themselves. It is questionable whether this was true of Tess's parents. They seemed to be continually engaged in a process of denying to each other significant parts of their being, giving appropriate conscious and unconscious justification of their enduring sacrifices in the marriage. Tess was left to a maid who rather ironically was called (in Spanish) "love." This allowed the static relationship between father and mother to continue undisturbed for a time. Tess's identification with her mother symbolically allowed her to be both her mother and herself. In this way unique feelings developed in Tess toward her father, her mother, and herself. Her mother denied Tess nurturance because she rejected in herself that part which Tess represented and because, at a later date, her intuition revealed that she had a rival in Tess. The father, needing his own reflection constantly mirrored in the sexuality of women, pulled Tess close. Later, he became frightened at the incestuous guilt. However, sexual fantasies were stimulated in Tess. In her psychotherapy, dreams and fantasies of "black and white" were prominent and recurred at certain stages in the treatment. Fantasies and dreams with such content are common in schizophrenics, and with Tess involved archaic images of purity and filth, of self-worth and abnegation, of creation and death, and other similar theses and antitheses. Tess symbolically recapitulated the encounter with her father in her relationship with me through the "black and white" medium. The basis for the ethical sense, diverted and distorted, was thereby restored.

While Tess had a highly developed verbal sense, a fine intellect, and widely variegated factual information to balance both, her communication was schizophrenic in its autistic and isolationistic qualities. Schizophrenic communication generally is not a constant but fluctuates from moment to moment. As the non-verbalized encounter with Tess became more meaningful, she would advance toward my communication system and I would retreat from hers. Later she could experience her being directly rather than through arcane symbols, body language, and similar nonconsensual methods. Tess' progress suggests that current conceptions of schizophrenic thinking, in terms of an abstract-concrete dichotomy, grossly oversimplify the question of schizophrenic mentation. A diagnosis cannot be made on this factor alone without divorcing thinking from the thinker.

The drawings which Tess made of a person show no gross deviations in body hierarchy but, rather, a primitivization and sexual confusion. These drawings represent late stages in the treatment and are therefore not highly conclusive. Of greater significance for therapy were the monkey fantasies. Self-fantasies became converted to conscious images of monkeys; thus depersonalized and dehumanized they were acceptable to her superego. Tess fantasied not only monkeys with elongated, enlarged genitals, but she displaced the genitalia from their customary location, giving them a primacy usually reserved for other parts of the body. This was also done with the head and breasts. Drawings of this kind were later followed by the pairing up of monkeys in grotesque sexual behaviors. The later drawings represented a higher form of body organization since now two bodies had to be matched organizationally and in rhythm.

It is my view that no successful treatment of a chronic schizophrenic can occur without a reorganization of the body image. The psychological concept of self is so minutely bound up with our conception of our organs and body that it is difficult to conceive of a holistic psychic-self with an incomplete body-self. It is simpler to measure the psychic self as, for example, by the Q technique; the body self, however, lies in the deeper layers of the unconscious, with archaic, primitive, and imaginal components, and is not often available for study. It is, nevertheless, very much the foundation of all higher level self-constructs and the therapist gradually but certainly becomes aware of it. While we know that there is an isomorphism principle operative here, too little attention has been given to this phase of schizophrenia.

Jung[4] mentions that the individual in his dissociated state needs a directing or ordering principle if he is to attain the goal of synthesis. Synthesis permits the harmony of the opposed or dialectical parts of the psyche, that is, the conscious and the unconscious, and includes the soma as the substrate of the ego. Each of the five vectors of schizophrenia contributes to synthesis in the personality, and each is related to the other factors in a dynamic balance. When these factors become united through the integrative process which

---

[4] Jung, C. G. *The Undiscovered Self.* Boston: Little, Brown, 1957.

therapy provides, the symptoms or defenses known as schizophrenia are no longer needed and the patient can cast them off. This comes about through the encounter of two people in the therapeutic situation in which each witnesses the existence of the other in a new and, hopefully, more promising world.

# CHAPTER 12

# Doria: Self-Repugnance and Self-Destruction

Doria's psychotherapy was approached with trepidation. Accepting a chronic hospitalized schizophrenic for long-term psychotherapy poses manifold problems, and in Doria's case, psychotherapeutic failure had been the rule in the past. I was unsure that I could offer her the total encounter she needed, because I was at the time attempting to work with newer treatment concepts. The selection of such a patient for treatment seems to depend upon considerations of the therapist more than it does upon the patient. The indifference of the chronic schizophrenic to psychotherapy is in part a below-conscious awareness of the circumscriptions and limitations set by the therapist's own unconscious. If the therapist cannot first reconcile the negative factors within himself, or if there is no hope of his doing so as the psychotherapy proceeds, he will be disappointed. For these reasons, I most often select patients like Doria from my therapeutic group where, in more limited circumstances, we come to know each other first. Generally, the selection of patients for long-term treatment cannot be precise. However, with such patients I sometimes know rather quickly, often in the first or second hour, that I want to be engaged. I look for a "presence," or readiness, in the patient which I very definitely sense or intuit. The patient must also have had some broad exposure to the world, so that the nuances of culture and social living are potentially meaningful, and this presumes some cognitive as well as feeling status. But this is not to be confused with positive or negative statements of schizoid or schizophrenic affect.

As is often true with such patients, Doria was widely read. During the therapy she made allusions to history, poetry, and literature. Despite her severe withdrawal and abysmal social relationships, the ferment of idea, symbol, image, and archetype in her unconscious was great, and this facilitated the treatment. Doria had been diagnosed as schizophrenic at a number of hospitals. Such diagnoses, however, are cross-sectional and catch the patient in a transitional phase. They are therefore to be interpreted only within the longitudinal, observational framework which is psychotherapy. Because of Doria's blatant schizophrenic symptomatology, there was never any question that she was a schizophrenic person. This diagnosis was confirmed by my work with her.

The following life-history material has been gathered from a variety of sources, including the patient and her family. It probably has more than the usual reliability for such data for in many instances it is cross-validated by several observers, and was developed longitudinally over a number of years.

Doria Mykonos, as I call her, is, at the time of writing, a thirty-one-year-old Caucasian female. She is married, has four children, and is a Protestant. Her children, all girls, are Jean, Jane, Mary, and Helen, ages nine, eight, two, and one, respectively.

Doria was born in the mid-west in 1928, and moved to a large city in that region after nine months. She lived there with her grandparents as well as her parents. This was the first of a series of moves that continued until age six when she was taken to a large city in northern California. She lived there with an aunt until she was twelve. These moves were apparently motivated by a certain restlessness on the part of one or another parent and by the inability of the father to earn a satisfactory livelihood during the depression. He sold books, billboards, and radio time, ran a doughnut shop, and participated in a variety of ventures. Despite these efforts, he failed to achieve commercial success. Doria later lived in several smaller California towns, and finally met her husband at a state college she attended for two years. They moved to a large university town where her husband completed his A.B. in English and worked toward teacher certification. He held several short-term posts as a high-school teacher. There were at least six moves in the next eight years, and it was toward the last of these, in 1956, that the patient dates her illness.

The patient describes the years she lived with her aunt (from six to twelve) as happy, but has little recollection of the earlier years, about which she makes a wry face. She said she was a "gifted" child, and my independent investigation of her school history revealed IQ's ranging from 127 up, with an invariable A-minus average in scholarship. Her achievement tended to drop as she progressed from elementary to high school and college. She felt that being "gifted" was important since her mother and father valued intelligence and she tried to compensate intellectually for the greater love extended to her brothers, particularly by the mother. She developed artistic interests, but her mother wanted a "happy housewife" type. Her parents encouraged her in sports which she disliked and did not approve of the people she associated with. She was very attached to her aunt, who subsequently died of cancer. Before her aunt's death her aunt began drinking heavily, a pattern which Doria was to repeat in each instance with her father and her husband.

The records indicate that delivery was spontaneous, normal, and that she was breast-fed until nine months. She was a good eater and was easily weaned. However, she was born after the death of a first son who was very much wanted, and there were no offspring for four years after Doria's birth. This was a source of disappointment to her parents. She was adored by the father who "spoiled" her. The parents reported that she cried a great deal, was irritable, and became a voracious eater. She reacted violently to the birth of the next sibling.

While in college Doria worked as a theater cashier, telephone operator, and in a cannery part time. She has not been employed since. She met her husband in 1947 and they eloped about a year and a half later. She was in love with him, but his feelings toward her have not been precisely ascertained. Doria's parents were not fond of him and opposed the match. Mr. Mykonos drank heavily, even during courtship, and Doria was aware of this. When intoxicated, he became sexually aggressive and physically abusive. She would attempt to run away, but her ideals would not permit her to acknowledge his deficiencies. His behavior became more symptomatic as the marriage progressed and he finally sought therapy at the university clinic. Because of the treatment he was able to discontinue drinking.

Mr. Mykonos, Doria's husband, is a short, dark man with an uncomfortable air of chronic weariness and abstraction. He obviously takes pride in his attire, but his clothes are shoddy and his grooming incomplete. Most often he is defensive or he removes himself by fantasy in a staring, catatonic-like way. In spite of his intelligence, he is in his own eyes an unsuccessful man. He has not been able to secure or retain teaching positions and he drives a taxicab or sells books part time.[1] He is at odds with his parents—he considers his mother exceptionally dominating—his parents-in-law, his wife, children, other authority figures, friends. He apparently expects a kind of homage and recognition from his wife which should substitute for the honor the world has failed to give him. He is frankly not interested at this time in assuming the economic burden of his family—the children are being cared for by the parents-in-law —and while he is ambivalent about his wife he is drawn to her. He volunteers that he is neurotic and finds it difficult to stay in one

[1] It is probably not by chance that the latter was also the sometime vocation of Doria's father.

place for long. On being asked about possible treatment goals for his wife, he is vague. He wants her to be as she was during the first two years of marriage, and for her to have her "self" back. When pressed, he mentions the stereotype of a "mature woman." Since his wife has been away from him for two years, I inquired about other women. He said he has "catted" around but that they *all want something more.* "Something deeply emotional?" I asked. "Yes," he responded with a shrug. One of his psychotherapists summarized his problem as follows:

The treatment focus was toward clarifying his long-standing dependency needs, his conflict with authority figures, and his erratic acting out with excessive drinking and extra-marital relationships in times of stress and anger. These problems were actively observed in the distorted and difficult relationships that he developed with his wife, his own parents, and in his working relations with employers. His ability to earn an adequate income in proportion to his own skill and capacities to meet the basic needs of his family were seriously affected.

Mr. Bloom, age fifty-five, Doria's father, is a large, bluff man who has a need to make his mark in the world every moment of his existence. He is highly verbal and there is a wide discrepancy between his learning and achievement. He is said to drink heavily and, indeed, became drunk when he had to come to his first family therapy meeting. In 1954 he was a patient in the same state hospital in which his daughter is now lodged, and he was diagnosed as having schizophrenia, undifferentiated form. The admission note reads:

This is a fifty-year-old white male who enters the hospital with a commitment history that his condition began suddenly about three weeks ago. He is delusional, not sleeping, overactive, laughing, rambling speech, and is suffering from many financial worries. Patient states that his wife had a gastrectomy a year ago and he has been worried about it. Furthermore, he has had low income. His wife requested that he come to the hospital. His account is very vague and circumstantial. He complains that "he is not equipped for any job"; he blames his failure

147

on the economic situation, and states that things at home are going "both ways." Patient's history of present illness is marked by its vagueness.

Mr. Bloom was the youngest of five children. His father, a brilliant lawyer who died at the age of seventy-nine, was inconsistent in his discipline, expected more from the child than he could give, and made him feel inadequate. Mr. Bloom's mother was lenient with her children and he was her favorite.

Mr. Bloom has deep psychosexual problems, problems with religion, and problems in interpersonal relationships. He said, for example, "I've had a great deal of sex problems; if I knew about sex I could rule the world," and again, "I'm a lover; I like bad people even, particularly when they don't kick me." Study in the hospital brought the following additional facets of the father's personality to light:

Patient has always been a very ambitious person, wanting to succeed in business. He is a perfectionist, wanting everything to work out according to plan. He enjoys organizing and taking over a new business. He becomes overenthusiastic and expands his business beyond its potentialities. He is not very good at managing money. Patient has been upset because of a loss of his business in 1942. He blames himself for his failure, feels he has let his family down. After his business failed, he stayed away from his home for nine months, went to another state and did not correspond with his family. The wife showed considerable understanding, saying that she felt he needed to be by himself if he wished it, and accepted him back when he returned without any comment. He gets along very well with his two older children. He is inclined to argue with the youngest boy, who mother states has a similar personality make-up to that of the father. The wife is a university graduate and taught school. Patient feels inferior to her because of her education, but she feels he is much better informed without a formal education.

Mrs. Bloom seems much less important that the husband in

148

the genesis of Doria's illness. Her perception of herself is of one perpetually holding her finger in the dike to prevent imminent collapse, and she has felt this way for many years. Undoubtedly she needs to be masochistic, and many of these needs are served by taking over Doria's children in a suffering way. Physically, she is a small, unkempt woman in whose presence I make the association "witch." As Doria regresses she comes to closely resemble her mother and improvement can be measured by the visual deviation from this image. There is an often overt antagonism between mother and daughter: Upon leaving family therapy one day Doria kissed her father on the lips, but she merely brushed her mother's cheek in a most casual fashion. Mrs. Bloom has often had to fill the economic gap in her family, which she has apparently done with little complaint. She feels trapped in a set of circumstances which she feels unable to change, like Doria, but she has compromised her existence, unlike Doria, in a set of defenses which she manages at a considerable personal sacrifice.

Doria's illness came at a period when the family situation was better than it had been for some time. They lived in a small town in southern California where her husband was teaching. He brought home a steady pay check and had stopped drinking; their home was nicely furnished and they seemed to be getting on. It was at this time, in March 1956, that Doria began having difficulty sleeping and became obsessed by the idea that she was dying. She grew tense and irritable and finally refused to leave the house. A few days before, while wheeling her child down the street, she had a severe panic reaction and felt that she could not reach home. She had strong feelings of being shriveled inside and felt that she was turning into a vegetable. She became severely depressed and said at that point, "Now I have everything that I wanted but myself."

Her symptoms continued unabated so that she and the children went to live with her parents while her husband remained at his teaching post. A psychiatrist recommended electroshock, and she received eight treatments on an outpatient basis. Things improved, and in September she decided to move with her husband to a university town where he could work for his M.A. Soon after, her symptoms returned in full flower. Her parents found her house uncared for and Doria in a high state of disorganization. After consultation, hospitalization was arranged at a medical school hospital in November.

Her mental status on admission was described as cooperative but depressed. She was anxious and tearful, and repeatedly asked, "Do you think anything can be done about this now?" She needed constant reassurance that her condition was not irreversible, and would frequently break out in tears and say that she was not whole and felt all shriveled up inside. It was all her fault and too late to do anything about it, she thought. Between her admission and discharge her behavior was essentially the same. The following quotation from the medical school summarizes it:

Since her admission and to the date of her discharge, her behavior has remained essentially the same. The patient's stream of talk is usually coherent, is frequently interrupted by repetitious questions mentioned above, and by repetition of the statement that she feels shrivelled up inside, or that she does not feel whole, or that she has half a head, etc. Her emotional status was that of a severe depression with blunted affect. At the time of discharge, her affect appeared more appropriate and the depression was not as marked. The only abnormal mental trends noted were the delusions mentioned, which are still present. She is and was well oriented and seemed to comprehend what was being said to her. There was no evidence of hallucinations, her judgment was poor, her past memory fair, but she has great difficulty concentrating, and is unable to repeat a simple story recited by the therapist. Her judgment and insight were and remain poor.

For five months at the medical school she was carried in psychotherapy with the addition of amytal interviews, which revealed nothing not already known, and methedrine. Following this she was given thorazine along with psychotherapy. She was unable to make use of the interviews and continually recited the somatic

150

delusion that she had only "half a head." Her behavior on the ward was one of almost complete disorganization: She had to be constantly reminded not to smoke in bed and to maintain her personal appearance and grooming. The organization of her thinking and her behavior improved slightly with the medication.

Her husband entered collaborative therapy and as he made progress Doria seemed to regress. This also operated reciprocally.

There is much we do not know and understand about this case, yet [Doria] consistently uses the interview hour to discuss her helpless, hopeless feelings about not being able to get well because she only has "half a head." Recently, since she has been told she is being discharged, she admits that she still has the delusion but she does not talk about it so much because it seems to irritate people. She remains a pitiful, helpless, hopeless, marginally organized female with a sloppily groomed, picked face which causes perennial scabs or sores. There are occasional periods when Doria seems more motivated to take care of herself and deal with her problems in a realistic manner, but these periods of time only last for a few days and she again slumps back into her old condition. There appears to be a strong element of secondary gain involved in her hospitalization which makes psychotherapy with her very difficult. Recently it has been discovered that [Doria] is now eighteen to twenty weeks pregnant, a fact which greatly distresses her, but seems to please her husband. Outside of the above-mentioned improvements, [Doria] still presents the picture of a sloppily groomed, poorly motivated schizophrenic female with the somatic delusion of having something missing, sometimes a distorted "half a head." Her general clinical impression has never changed markedly throughout her two years' stay in the hospital. It is the general consensus of opinion [staff] that this woman is severely ill, has been, and probably will be ill chronically for a very long time, and that she has not responded adequately to the more permissive attitude of therapy present in this hospital. . . .

Doria then came to the state hospital where I first met her. The clinical picture was not dissimilar from that reported above. Her ward psychiatrist and a fellow patient on the ward who was in

151

group therapy with her prepared vignettes of Doria as they saw her soon after admission. The impression of the psychiatrist is as follows:

[Doria Mykonos] has been known to me for a year; during the past several months I have been her ward doctor. These rounds should be distinguished from a formal clinical evaluation in that they are candid and less thorough. I first noticed the patient on the admission service. Her face was abraded in many areas; her grooming was careless and unattractive; her walk was fluid and smooth but somehow disagreeable; her manner indicated indecision, preoccupation, and indifference to others; she wept or laughed or looked blank but she communicated no urgency nor was her affect contagious. She impressed me as being unappealing or even repulsive and I wondered at the solicitude others seemed to feel toward her. Later, as her ward doctor, my attitude changed little except that in persistent rule-breaking she became a nuisance, comparable to a low-grade chronic ache. I never felt I could communicate with her, to really get through to her; in contrast to my reaching most other patients. I felt no urgency about helping her. In these ways she stood out as different from other patients.

The fellow patient's description presents her in this way:

There sitting on the smoking porch of the ward in the rocking chair, staring out into space with unseeing eyes—yes it's a woman—yet not a woman. More dead than alive. She doesn't care either for herself or the child she carries. Her eyes are dull to this time and place. Now and then they flicker with fires of some other hell—her private hell. The phantoms dance before her eyes in all their shadowy horror, obscuring from sight the world in which she occupies space and time. She digs her face and head until it's a bloody pulp. She burns holes in her clothes—slopping ashes and coffee abundantly over herself and the floor until everybody retreats. Minutes later she pulls herself from the chair and slops over to the group—leans over me, takes the cigarette from my hand to light her own—knocking the fire from mine. Then flops on the sofa and commences to breathe down the neck of the girl laying there reading the paper. Minutes pass, the group becomes aware of a vague irritation—it's there again—haunting them—if only it would go away and evaporate into nothingness. If only it was a fly—they could swat it and relieve themselves of further agitation. "What" she repeats. One of the group, suppressing their hostility, explains what has transpired. "Why" she mumbles with apparent disinterest. Hostility mounts within the group—they are tense and mute. They disband, running from their own feelings. She is glad—glad they don't like her—glad that she doesn't like them—glad they are alone now, like she is. She's tested them and they have failed—like she has failed. The world is hate and hate is the world.

I have already given my own impressions of the patient and of her impact upon me. I did not feel the repulsion reported by the ward doctor and other patients. I saw only the potentialities for her growth and for an altered existence, and I was willing to make a commitment which would throw us together in an extended psychotherapeutic relationship. I never wavered from this commitment, but I had two periods in which I became mildly disinterested in her, with serious but transient repercussions. Such patients, it seems, must always be treated counter to the hospital's subtly negative and unfavorable prognostications, a pessimism that goes with chronic schizophrenia and the tremendous number of patients who need to be reached. No presentation can do justice to the nuances which occur in the psychotherapy of a schizophrenic patient. My course will be to sample certain aspects of the treatment which clearly demonstrate and illustrate my theoretical viewpoints. Treatment involves individual psychotherapy, group therapy, and family therapy.[2] The patient was seen from two to five hours a week for approximately 360 hours, and approximately 35 additional hours of group and family therapy were given.

In the analysis of schizophrenic existence the emphasis is on the here-now, on the dynamic interpersonal field. This field comes eventually to mirror all the facets of the ego in its many layers and in its cultural boundedness. This approach does not ignore the his-

[2] Co-therapist in family therapy was Arthur Anderson, M.D.

torical or the unconscious, since an ego without its development is meaningless. Rather, history is put in the service of the intercurrent, so that the world-design of the patient can be reformulated on a new choice basis. Regardless of the possibility of a schizophrenogenic mother or father, the patient can choose her life. Technically, this point of view is subject to several hazards, not the least of which is over-simplicity. Obviously, the patient cannot make an intellectual choice to be different. If she could, she would not need to be treated. This choice can only come about through the encounter and its transference. The therapeutic problem is described by a quotation from Binswanger.[3]

The temporality of this world was one of *urgency* [italics his] . . . its spatiality therefore one of horribly crowded narrowness and closeness, pressing upon "body and soul" of the existence. . . . All this could be demonstrated not only in the modes and changes of spatiality, of the hue, materiality, and dynamics of the various worlds, but also in the modes and changes of temporality, up to the state of the "eternal emptiness" of so-called autism.

The patient must become temporal rather than atemporal; spatiality, that is, object values, must assume new meanings; emptiness or loneliness must become pregnant, and crowdedness less obsessive and oppressive. This can be done if the basic conflict of the Absurd can be resolved. Spatiality and temporality are relatives operating within a framework of meaning. Without such meaning they are physical aspects leading to Nothingness, to arbitrary or sick usages. At our stage of knowledge of the psychotherapy of schizophrenia the relationship between a specific patient and a specific therapist is more determinative than technique, and it sometimes appears as though improvement is actually unrelated to technique. There are some new departures in technique in my treatment, but

[3] Binswanger, L. "The Existential Analysis School of Thought." In May, R., *et al.* (Eds.). *Existence, A New Dimension in Psychiatry and Psychology.* New York: Basic Books, 1958, pp. 206, 209.

they are secondary to the encounter itself, which can be verbalized only with difficulty.

The existence therapy of schizophrenia differs from other approaches largely in theoretical or philosophical outlook. Thus, in the case of Doria, I talk about transference and countertransference factors, of the analysis of unconscious productions, resistance, interpretation of feelings, and many other concepts which are used in classical psychoanalysis. What does distinguish this approach from others, however, is the emphasis on the patient's own world and world-design and the therapist's need to enter and share it in a way not often done with psychotics; the determinative choice the patient has not only of her symptoms but of the world she wishes to make; the valuative and relativistic nature of temporality and spatiality that causes "meaning" to assume a prominent place in the illness and its genesis; the regressive and symbolic efforts to reconcile Nothingness and the Absurd not only in the developmental history of the person but in the history of all people and culture. The emphasis is on a new drama of life with the psychotherapist in the present (with implications of past and future) in which a new mode of existence must be found. This does not exclude contemporary psychoanalytical techniques if the fundamental conditions of treatment can be met. However, meeting these conditions usually results in some alterations in conventional techniques, or at least in the uniformity with which they are applied.

The transference is only one aspect of the encounter, but it is the one we know most about. In the past we have used this concept loosely to describe the entire interpersonal relationship between patient and therapist. This is incorrect, for there is a conscious "living together" in the psychotherapy which is not necessarily transference, and in psychotics, much of the magical-animistic content of thinking seems primordial beyond the usual transference functions. In fact, it is often difficult to distinguish between these contents, since they superimpose and overlap and have a special relationship to each other. Any psychotherapy of a schizophrenic which stops with the analysis of a classical transference will miss both the import of the ego relationship between the patient and therapist, and the contributions of the deeper past. In the discussion which follows, these separate contributions have not been kept distinct; it is important, however, to be aware of their separate natures.

I divide the transference phenomena arbitrarily into first, second, and final stages, recognizing that these are not equal in a time sense. The first stage involves establishing the encounter and the clarification of the problem to be solved. This is most often the most difficult phase because past therapeutic failure and chronicity have been reinforced and delusional and other defenses set. The manifold and distorted resistances of the schizophrenic to psychotherapy are, of course, now well known. During this stage the patient tests the commitment of the therapist to her in diverse ways while she also tests the double-bind propensities of the therapist's world-design. The therapist must respond with a consistent, loving, and open relatedness and provide a "new" mother prepared to welcome her infant. Countertransferences are often maximal in this stage, for the demands are exorbitant, the pace slow, and the therapist has a need to cure quickly. His own reality, and what is schizophrenic in him, is challenged, so that his anxiety, hostility, and other defensive mechanisms are convenient but troublesome devices. In the most critical moments the therapist re-emphasizes his dedication. If it is not harmful to the patient, he reveals his own feelings or impulses which are blocking the "growth together" of the encounter. The work here is often nonverbal, and sometimes nursing may be needed.

The middle transference phase is redolent more of the neurotic than the psychotic. The transference has been established and the patient has accepted herself as ill, at least for the purpose of treatment. She gives the therapist limited permission to look at her defenses, and she will test the reality of the therapeutic hour as well as hours away from therapy. Her anxiety waxes and wanes and becomes more available for analysis and growth. It is possible now to work with symbols on a verbally interpretive level rather than in the deeper layers. The encounter now assumes historical, that is, mother and father, projections, as well as here-now properties. Implications for the future appear faintly and the patient voices a note of optimism. The transference is at its height.

The final phase is the disengagement of the encounter. The patient has less need of the therapist's ego and is well on the way to an existence in which the Absurd and Nothingness are assumed as a burden of life and do not encourage anxiety of a pan sort. This phase may be lengthy because the schizophrenic needs life-support for a longer period than the neurotic. Practical problems may also arise with her family when she returns to them. This is an area of difficulty for the psychotherapist because he too must experience relinquishment, and the final points in such a relationship are not so clearly demarcated in our knowledge as the beginnings.

If I may borrow an image from Camus, I would say that schizophrenia is "like a plague. One craves human contacts but one never knows when one is infected. It is precisely at the moment when one feels safe or free that one finds his life snatched from him."[4] Doria reacted to our opening meetings as though she feared she would be infected with plague. She had invested considerable energy in a system which convinced her that she was unliked and unloved, and she had considerable family and community support for this belief. Her scabrous face and her insistence that half her head, the thinking, intellectual part, was missing made denial of a relationship easy for her. Indeed, her constant whining repetition of this "programed" material made it difficult to love her consistently, if at all. I was content to accept her face-picking and head-delusion for many hours, and when crises occurred I reiterated my commitment to her. If she did not come to me, I went to her. She would often come late or not come at all, and had the usual repertory of schizophrenic testing behavior: She would oscillate between almost total nihilism and an exuberant giving over to me of complete responsibility for her self. Comments such as these were frequent: "I don't know where everything went." "My husband needs

---

[4] Camus, A. *The Plague.* London: Hamish Hamilton, 1957, p. 78.

me but he can't have me until I have myself." "I don't know how to be useful anymore." "You have to help me. My children are growing up. It is your responsibility."

The turning point came probably when I offered to visit her in a general hospital when she delivered the child she was carrying. Thereafter she would occasionally come to the hours with a slightly less blemished face and with some piece of personal adornment. She became more regular in her appointments and more autobiographical. During the hour, she would need to "destroy," and she regularly shredded the matches I made available for her cigarettes. I made no demands on her and gave no interpretations, but I did begin to say that people did have a choice about their lives. When she scratched her face in my presence, I offered her my hand to hold. I did this each time she scratched. After several rejections, she took my hand and squeezed it warmly, and the scratching in the subsequent hours gradually diminished. Much later I told her that she did not need to "destroy" and refused to give her the matches after lighting her cigarettes. This limit-setting was salubrious, for she was fearful of her own omnipotence and of the possibility of destroying me.

At this time I asked her to paint one hour a week and set aside a secluded place in which she could work. Later she changed to modeling in clay. She was also given a work assignment in the employees' dining room, but the employees complained that the scabs she picked fell into the food and she was dismissed. Her creative activity was particularly rewarding because being creative was an important need for her, and her productions were proof of her retained capacities. In addition to making symbolic and archetypal material available for discussion, they challenged the vacuum she thought she had in her head. Gradually she began to question the organic basis for her "missing head," rejecting chemical, metabolic, and other structural theories. She now talked of a missing "function"; however, there were frequent regressions. One day she came to the hour without a blemish on her face; and on another day she was very attractive in a new dress and high-heeled shoes. At the same time, severe acting-out occurred at the ward level, so that ward personnel became unhappy with her and she had to be returned to a closed ward. She seemed to do better for a while, from the institutional point of view, when protection of this kind was afforded her.

At this time she met a male patient in the hospital and began a friendship of some intensity with him. I watched this "enthusiastically" since it was the first of her nontherapeutic investments of some moment in another person, and it helped to establish her as valuable in her own eyes. It served also to provide some "transference distance" at the moments when it was needed in the treatment. However, she also attempted to use this man to provoke me, for example, by establishing her courting place with him under my window.

It was more or less at this point that she began a studied effort to understand her past in terms of its contribution to her present state and consented to write her autobiography. The impetus in part was my reading of Walter Lowrie's *A Short Life of Kierkegaard* which she saw on my desk. She asked to borrow the book and read it in the following week. At this time, also, a former patient who had been previously hospitalized for schizophrenia and whom I had treated came with her child to visit me. She met Doria and invited her to her home. Doria wanted to know in precise detail how ill she had been and could not accept the fact that the visitor now was well. However, the visitor served as an example of a new successful existence and was frequently referred to in later hours.

Conceptually, some of the dynamic material of Doria's case can be organized in a limited, threefold scheme as follows: first, Mind-bind; second, Judgment; and third, Individuality.

*Mind-bind.* Doria's most prominent symptom was her delusion that she had only "half a head." She clung tenaciously to this belief and nothing heretofore had changed it. From this stemmed her second prominent symptom. She vigorously picked her face to reassure herself unconsciously that her head was still there. This was a core defense maintained against all evidence to the contrary.

159

I call this the mind-bind problem because in family therapy Doria equated the two by a slip of the tongue, saying "bind" when she meant "mind."

For every schizophrenic there is one family member who assumes special importance. If the father or mother, as the case may be, does not have a direct part in the Either/Or conflict he or she is at least instrumental in keeping it in force. Children have a need to be like one parent and to exceed him. The former is possible in ways we now understand, but the latter is fraught with great hazard for the child. The parent we call schizophrenogenic will not allow himself to be surpassed at any cost although he actually seduces the child into a kind of unhealthy competition. This competition provides for the parent's own worth.

The evidence in this case is that it is the father who is most important to Doria. We know that Mr. Bloom was hospitalized as schizophrenic, so there is no question as to his schizophrenogenic possibilities. It appears that he has maintained his own precarious existence outside the hospital through Doria's illness. In family therapy he is the most adamant that Doria is ill and needs to be kept in the hospital, all evidence to the contrary. From his own experiences as an ill person, one would expect the reverse to be true. Doria's youngest child is his favorite and he is deeply involved with her, just as he was with Doria. He has found a surrogate for Doria, one closer at home, but he also has Doria. Because of this child he may yet be able to release Doria from his hidden bondage; without her it might appear hopeless. It is significant that as she has improved he has found it necessary to find work away from home.

Doria wants to reinstate the symbiotic and seductive relationship she had with her father when she was at one with him and could exceed him. Her existence was clear then, as was her sexuality. Above all he values the "head," that is, the intellect. The "head" is the source of all strength and creation; it is what makes a man and compensates for all inadequacies. The Bloom family as a whole is distinguished by scholarship despite the paucity of economic resources. Mr. Bloom, although deficient himself, values the intellectual prowess of Doria's children. He is thus following a familiar pattern. Furthermore, this is also the distinguishing hallmark of Mr. Mykonos, Doria's husband. It is the "head" and not the "body" that counts with him, and when this is missing his inner world collapses. Doria was found to be significantly lacking in body-image conception and body-image language. This occurs also in children whose ego was never given the opportunity of maturation, and the failure to find the "body" is characteristic of those who have difficulty in interpersonal relationships.

Through therapeutic activity with clay Doria was able to recover her body from neck to midsection and showed significant promise of the rest to come. She is now more than a "head," and for the first time body integration is a possible reality. An image of a Balinese dancer which she made demonstrated this. Particularly significant for interpersonal relationships in this figure are the prominent breasts and nose.

The double-binds in which children who become schizophrenic find themselves are extremely complex, and no simple formula does them justice. Doria's principal double-bind situation was the conflict of emotion and intellect, which became the Either/Or conflict. She had to give up her existential destiny for unity with her father, whose adhesive was a kind of perverse love. Later something similar was sought and perpetuated with the husband. In therapy we have clarified this to the point where Doria has insight into it and recognizes it as one basis for her negation of life.

Since the process of undoing such a double-bind involves more than Doria herself, the entire family—Doria, husband, mother, father—have been meeting with two therapists one hour a week as a group. This has been a comparatively late but very profitable development in Doria's treatment. Originally, getting the family together seemed an impossibility, so that Doria participated, with seven other patients, in group therapy two hours a week with me alone. Members of the group became family surrogates, and she was able to work out some of the "mind-bind" problem here. Now direct confrontation of her father and husband is possible in the family

161

group, so that less symbolic and more actual realization is possible. In these groups the undoing of the mind-bind problem has begun. They have made it possible to determine the family dynamics more accurately and to offer it to the reality consensus of the family. Within such a framework, unconscious needs resulting in double-binds can be clarified in a way not otherwise possible with schizo-phrenics.

*Judgment.* Most schizophrenics feel they are being judged. This is not unusual, since all Western men carry such a sense of be-ing judged. For schizophrenics, however, the judgment is critical and they go through life as what Camus calls judge-penitents.[5] Judgment is a result of the schizophrenic's need to be and the guilt they have for this need. Thus Doria repeated many times that she wanted to be like others yet she picked her face so that her distinc-tion made her unequal. Equality is a need for a special position in relationship to the self and to others. The schizophrenic is more deeply engaged in life than other people, witness, for example, his need for love, and his need to offer it, so that interpersonal factor is more critical and basic trust a matter of the greatest moment. Thus Doria needs to be more than equal, and she cannot settle for equal-ity alone. With Doria, as with others, fantasy, legend, and myth, all reveal the need for a powerful position in relationships with people. Humility is a very rare theme in such productions.

A judge-penitent is one who suffers endlessly without either the transcendent quality which suffering brings or the expected so-cial response to it. It is thus a meaningless act of self-judgment and punishment. Its senselessness and continuity are such that temporal-spatial values applied to it also become meaningless. It is as though the schizophrenic must continually punish himself not for living, as we formerly thought, but, more properly, for his extraordinary aspirations toward life. The problem in therapy is to relate the suf-fering to some interpersonal framework so that grandiosity will be given up for the human burden we all share. Doria first came to

[5] Camus, A. *The Fall.* New York: Knopf, 1957.

recognize her suffering as suffering, then to relate it to the framework of both of us, and finally to put it into the service of her growing ego.

*Individuality.* A common theme with Doria was her need for privacy. She constantly felt invaded and needed to withdraw. This need for privacy is often seen in people who have desperate needs for contact. The paradox occurs because one feels that something is lost or taken away in human interaction and if one goes too far with it one may be totally lost. Schizophrenics do not see themselves as containing anything, that is, they feel they are empty. This is because their ego boundaries are ill defined and their personality at the mercy of the world. It can be demonstrated that as the container properties of the person become more fixed and definite, the need for privacy vanishes.

In the treatment, the patient's desire for privacy is respected and no encroachment upon it is made. The two conflicting needs war with each other and it is a serious mistake for the therapist to take sides too early. A fine balance must be preserved until the patient comes to feel that she can contain something. After the point had been reached where Doria read and discussed Kierkegaard's life with me, she was able to retain more within her boundaries. This was gradual, indicated by the sculpture, drawings, and paintings she did.

Otto Will, in describing the psychotic person, says, "The child does not view the world as does the usual adult, nor does the poet. The psychotic person is not a child, and is not always a poet, but he seems at times like both, and we who listen to him feel frustrated as we recognize how bound we are by our conventional frame of reference." In order to treat Doria it was necessary to know both the poet and infant in her. The former operates on the level of images and symbols, the latter by direct uncomplicated action. The poetic aspect is probably best revealed by modalities which tap the several layers of the unconscious unfettered by the rules of logic. Through painting, sculpture, and written productions, the poet and infant were disclosed and unified.

163

Her final paintings presaged things to come. As her treatment continued she lost more and more of her estrangement, reached out toward other people, and insisted on leaving the hospital. Her improvement was not matched by growth on the part of her family who had considerable unconscious investment in the maintenance of her illness. In family therapy she was finally able to confront her father and husband with her needs as a person and to point out logically the part they themselves played in her illness. At this point the husband told of his ambivalence about resuming his life with her outside the hospital and began drinking again. Mr. Bloom still maintains that she needs to be in the hospital, but he is less firm in his position. Treatment continues on all fronts, but it is now less intensive. Doria no longer has the delusion about her head, her face is picked only in times of great regressive stress, and she is ready for what life offers outside of the protection of a hospital.

In view of earlier therapeutic failure, it seems to me that the significant contribution of therapy was to recognize the existential problems in Doria's life and to help her to choose a different and better world in relation to her time and space. The patient has now been out of the hospital for approximately ten years. She and her husband have continued with group therapy in sporadic bursts, but in general are more self-sufficient and happier. The patient shows none of the psychotic symptoms for which she was originally hospitalized.

She recently phoned (January 1967) to say that she has an excellent administrative position in the Economic Opportunity Program, has remained married to her husband, and has had a successful but distant rapprochement with her father and mother.

# Acknowledgments

Most of the chapters in *Modern Humanistic Psychotherapy* have been previously published by me in various journals. However, for this book they have all been rewritten or totally edited. Chapter 2, "Schizophrenia and Existence," appeared in *Psychiatry*, 1960, *23*, 385–394, under the same title. It is reprinted with the permission of the William Alanson White Psychiatric Foundation. Chapter 3, "Schizophrenic Temporality," was originally published as "The Moment in Psychotherapy," in the *American Journal of Psychoanalysis*, 1960, *20*, 41–48. It is used with their permission. "Loneliness as Schizophrenia," Chapter 4, was similarly published as "On the Nature of Loneliness," in the *American Journal of Psychoanalysis*, 1961, *21*, 34–39. They have given permission to the use of it here. Chapter 5, "The Meaning of the Transference," appeared as "Beyond the Transference," in *Psychotherapy: Theory, Research, Practice*, 1964, *1*, 49–53. Permission to use it here has been granted. "Therapeutic Interruption," Chapter 6, was first printed as "Therapeutic Interruption: Planned and Unplanned," in the *American Journal of Psychoanalysis*, 1966, *26*, 81–87. I have their permission to use it here. Chapter 7, "Acting-Out Behavior," appeared in the same journal under the title of "The Transference and Countertransference of Acting-Out Behavior," 1965, *25*, 79–84. Permission to reprint it here has been granted. Chapter 8, "Artistic Productions in Psychotherapy" was a chapter in *The Use of Written Productions in Counseling and Psychotherapy*, edited by Leonard Pearson and published in 1965 by C C Thomas, Springfield, Illinois. The editor and publisher have given permission to use it here. Chapter 9, "Touching the Patient as Mothering" was first titled "The Touching of the Body," *Psychoanalytic Review*, 1964, *51*, 122–134. Robert E. Kantor collaborated in it. Permission to present it here has been granted. Chapter 10, "Fear of Death as Countertransference," was called "Death as a Countertransference" and similarly appeared in the *Psychoanalytic Review*, 1963, *49*, 1–20. I have permission to reprint. Chapter 11, "Tess: Flight from Caritas," originally appeared in a book I edited, *Case Studies in Counseling and Psychotherapy*, published by Prentice-Hall in 1959. They have given permission to use it here. The final chapter, 12, "Doria: Self-Repugnance and Self-Destruction," was published in still another book I edited, *Psychotherapy of the Psychoses*, Basic Books, 1961, under the title "The Quest for the Golden Mean: A Study in Schizophrenia." Basic Books has given permission to use it here.

# Index

apeutic Analyzers, 66–67; Therapeutic Synthesizers, 67

Psychotherapy: acting-out behavior in, 71–79; attitude of therapist, 51–52; body contact in, 92–105; creativity in, 80–83; de–emphasis on pregenital period, 51–52; emphasis on intercurrent situation, 51–52; entry in, 36–37; erotic overtones in, 102–103; exit in, 37; extra-transferential aspects, 49; interruption of, 60–70; interval-therapy, 85–86; invincibility and omnipotence feelings as deterrents in, 121–123; limits of, 50–51; long-term, selection of patients, 60–64; in marital counseling, 89–90; "moment of truth" in, 35–36; passivity and femininity of, 74–75; referral in, 64–65; synthesis in, 141–142; in terms of (a) the Eros Quotient, 57–58, (b) the Eros/Thanatos Quotient, 57–58, (c) the Good-Bad Dialogue, 53–56, (d) the Other, 56–57; therapist's personality factors, 24–27, 64–69; time in, 28–38; transference in, 49–59, 62–63, 78, 102–103, 155–157; use of diaries, 88–91; "written productions" in, 80–91

**R**

REDLICH, F. C., 81
Referral, 64–65

ROGERS, C. R., 57
ROSEN, J., 50, 99

**S**

SARTRE, J.-P., 2, 31, 45
SCHEFFLEN, A. E., 99
SCHILDER, P., 16
Schizophrenia (*see also* Schizophrenic): as avoidance of the Absurd, 17–21, 25–27; defensive aspects of, 12–17; diagnostic types, 44; existence therapy of, 6–7, 155; illustrative case histories of (a) flight from love, 127–142, (b) self-repugnance and self-destruction, 143–164; individuality in, 163; judgment in, 162–163; limiting factors in therapy, 23–24; in literature, 17–23, 44–45; loneliness in, 39–46; mind-bind problem in, 159–162; need for privacy, 163; as Nothingness or Non-Being, 2–6; perversion of time in, 33–34; philosophy of life, 1–2; repression of creativity and spontaneity as cause, 76–78; self-concept in, 5–6, 15–17, 53–56, 95–96; Self-Other Dialogue in, 3, 40–41; therapist and patient, intercommunication, 24–27

Schizophrenic (*see also* Schizophrenia): body image of, 15–17, 56; communication impairment, 13–14; double-binds in, 21, 159–162; ethical sense of, 14–15; interpersonal phenom-